CHRIST AND CRISIS

CHRIST AND CRISIS

by

CHARLES MALIK

University Professor at The American University, Washington, D.C.; Professor of Philosophy at the American University of Beirut, Lebanon; and Former President of the General Assembly of the United Nations.

Wm. B. Eerdmans Publishing Company,   Grand Rapids, Mich.

To the loving memory of
My Grandmother

who first taught me
with tears
the Everlasting Faith

CONTENTS

FOREWORD

I

This book contains seven Christian meditations on the state of the world. By "Christian" here is meant, not only that the person who has undertaken these meditations is Christian, but that the world itself is expressly viewed as somehow under the judgment of Jesus Christ. Entirely apart from any Christian, and certainly apart from the meditation of any Christian, there is a world in crisis, and the crisis is simply the fact that Jesus Christ is the Lord and is judging. *Krinein* means to separate, to winnow, therefore to distinguish and discriminate, therefore to judge. There is a vast *separating*, a profound *crisis,* going on, both in individual lives — above all in the lives of Christians — and in the world at large. *What* is being *separated*? *What* is being *judged*? What is the *principle,* the *criterion,* according to which the separating and the judging is taking place? *Who* is doing the separating and the judging? Is it a spontaneous, blind, automatic, natural *drift* of an otherwise self-sufficient world? Or is the "judge" something *over against* this world, so that apart from this independent judge the world cannot be in crisis nor can it ever judge itself? These are questions that haunted the writer at every step in these meditations, and the reader is begged to keep them in mind. What is affirmed is that, at its deepest levels, the crisis is *caused* by Jesus Christ, in the half a dozen different senses of the term "cause." This thesis is not fully elaborated in these pages; it is for the most part implied; here and there it is only hinted at; it is certainly a fundamental presupposition of the whole argument; its most explicit — though still exceedingly preliminary — treatment is found in Chapter IV; but the author has in mind to elaborate it at length in another work.

I ask the reader: Are you perplexed? Do you "feel" the crisis? Do you "feel" something profoundly wrong, both in your life and in the affairs of the world? Do you as it were "hold your heart in your hand," fearing that almost the next moment something terrible is going to break out — *both in you and in the world?* Have you reached the state where you simply do not quite trust the processes of the world (including nature, science, economics, politics and even the best good will), suspecting that there is in them a flaw somewhere, a false note, an immanent principle of darkness, destruction and death vitiating everything *at some stage* (e.g., when a system you painstakingly built up collapses, or when a friendship you nursed with your heart and tears goes to pieces, or when you die)? If such is the state of your mind, both with respect to yourself and to the world, then what these meditations are suggesting is that, if you turn with all your heart to Jesus Christ, on your knees, in the Bible, in the communion of saints throughout history, in your moments of absolute contemplation, in the great tradition, and above all in the Church, it is more certain than any mathematical proof that He will show you, not only *why* the perplexity and the crisis and the wrong and the flaw and the awful uncertainty of the moment, but *how* to overcome, *in Him,* all this havoc of the devil. In the life of the spirit the first principle is freedom; thus there is nothing fatalistically determined here; everything depends on the "if you turn with all your heart to Jesus Christ." Nothing will be revealed to you, and Christ in the crisis will ever remain an impenetrable mystery to you, if not downright nonsense and irrelevance, until you freely comply with this tremendous "if."

II

But if freedom is the first principle of the spirit, faith and trust is the second, and patience the third. When the present writer affirms that in Jesus Christ you will understand the crisis and overcome it, clearly he is in very good company. This is not an original discovery of his; Paul said it before, so did Augustine and the Saints. Why therefore should you not trust this immense "cloud of witnesses?" Some of these men and women had as much fun in life, knew as much science and philosophy, discharged as much responsibility to their generation, were as much human and good, as any atheist or agnostic or cynic or skeptic or materialist or socialist or nationalist in this unhappy age. When with one voice they witness to Jesus Christ, a strong *prima facie* evidence exists that there is something in what they say. They have no "axe" to grind; they attach no "strings" to their witness; they entertain no "ulterior" motives; they are simply and purely expressing what they know and believe. If what they say is not in itself compelling, it is at least interesting and even arresting. Certainly you are absolutely at liberty not to believe in them; but then you are also at *liberty to believe* in them. And if you do not believe, then two questions arise: (a) why don't you trust them, seeing that their witness is so simple, so unaffected, so disinterested, so detached, so pure?; something must repel you in them, something must be repugnant to you — what is it?; and (b) what then do you believe, *whom do you trust?* These are searching questions, for no man believes nothing, and every man must have a reason for what he believes.

How to overcome the petty and unworthy in one's own life, with laughter and dance and joy; how to rise above fears and hesitations and the calculating wit; how not to prejudge; how not to let "sociological" considerations obscure the truth; how to have a pure and open heart; how to be a child; how to be born anew; how to be "moved" by the sight and witness of the pure; how to trust the trustful and profit to the utmost from "the benefit of the doubt"; how to listen and then hear when truth and being speak; how to *see being* — simply, humbly, thankfully, perhaps at times with tears; how to *love the sight of being,* and therefore to be seeking it day and night — above every blessing in life, blessed is the man who prays for these things, and, before he dies, acquires a measure of them.

III

You suspect there is something, somehow you are moved; therefore you believe. The "suspecting" and the "being moved" never take place in a vacuum: they are the result of *meeting* (in Buber's sense of the term) a living person who himself believes and has found. Faith passes from person to person, from life to life. When it clicks, nobody knows; but no personal meeting, then certainly no faith. And nothing is greater in life than to trust the trustworthy and trusting.

Having freely believed because of your living contact

with the faithful and trustworthy, you must then be patient with your faith. Give it a chance. There is a peculiar law of life and growth about faith. It will be tried every day of your life, and as it is tried, it develops and deepens and matures. The Biblical doctrine of patience is fundamental. We are told of "the patience and the faith of the saints" (Revelation 13:10 and 14:12); we are also told to "glory in tribulations . . . : knowing that tribulation worketh patience; and patience, experience; and experience, hope" (Romans 5:3-4; see also Luke 8:15, Colossians 1:11-12, James 1:3-4 and *passim*). Thus there is absolutely no magic in our life with God: we must traverse the whole gamut of human suffering and trial; and "he that shall endure unto the end, the same shall be saved" (Matthew 24:13 and Mark 13:13). And when we catch the faith of the saints, we must give our faith time, in all patience and longsuffering, before Jesus Christ reveals Himself to us as *the cause and the meaning* of the crisis of our life and the crisis of the world.

IV

The present writer is neither a minister nor a priest nor a bishop nor an apostle: he is a simple layman. He therefore speaks, in the words of Kierkegaard, "without authority." But when is a layman forbidden or prevented from pondering himself and the world in the presence and the light of Jesus Christ? If Jesus Christ is real in a man's life, how can he help seeing the world through Him? The present writer saw what he saw and came to the conclusions to which he came in the thick of the trials of life. Not a word, not a comma, written in this book was conceived in the abstraction of thought. Always the totality of human personal existence was at stake — in the crucible of the judgment of Christ. He understands nothing of the life of the Christian who thinks that it is a question of ideas, and one wonders if the theologians who are perpetually engaged in the "systematic" balancing of ideas really know what it is all about. The greatest systematic theologian of all time was perhaps Thomas Aquinas; and yet something mysterious happened to him at the end of his life while he was celebrating Mass which made him absolutely disgusted with his writings, and he said to a friend of his who was urging him to go on writing, "I can write no more. I have seen things which make all my writings like straw." What did he see? — nobody knows; but I often think that perhaps he suddenly realized in prayer that all his stupendous theologizing and systematizing was one unrelieved act of intellectual pride, when all that was needed was to love and trust God like a child. Posterity can not be grateful enough that he was vouchsafed that humbling vision only *after* he had completed his great work, because endless good and "use" has nevertheless flowed from what he was led at the end to look upon as "straw." So long as we possess this inquiring intellect, we must use it to the full, and use it aright, especially as it belongs to our glory as beings created in the image and likeness of God; and *intellectually speaking,* provided we are always spiritually on our knees acknowledging our creaturehood and our sin, there is no better guide in matters theological than Saint Thomas. But such was the goodness of God, especially to those who came after Saint Thomas, that, *after* the Saint had faithfully and safely deposited his incomparable intellectual achievement, he was shown something incomparably greater still, precisely perhaps as a sort of reward for the momentous exertions and achievements of his intellect. One often wonders whether it was an accident that Socrates and Christ never wrote a word. Life and being always come first, and while one *is fully living,* in absolute responsibility and wholeness and irony and fun, he simply *has no time* for writing and systematizing.

Thus there is cleverness, meaninglessness, hollowness, pride, self-envy, estrangement, struggle, suffering, sin, rebellion, filth, misery, despair, the devil, the fall, the sweetness of scheming, the torrent of words, the death which one faces in absolute loneliness, "the imaginations of the thoughts," terror, blasphemy, cursing God; and there is purity, wholeness, truth, transparency, simplicity, trust, strength, victory, power, tears, joy, speechlessness, freedom, creativity, vision, identity with God, grace, peace, Jesus Christ; and he has no right to *think* of these things, much less to *expound* them, who does not know them on the razor edge of his living death and his dying life. Despite its talking about all sorts of "worldly" things, very worthy and very important, this book must be understood in every word of it as primarily, if largely indirectly, attempting to articulate, under certain limitations and in the diverse perspectives of the moment, the wrestling of actual, existing, living, poor man with the devil who is relentlessly trying to pull him down to utter nothingness, a wrestling nevertheless carried out in the presence and with the power of God who created actual, existing, living, poor man out of sheer nothingness, and who, for some mysterious reason, has not yet willed to obliterate the devil to absolute nothingness. And in this wrestling Jesus Christ smashes the ugly head of the devil with His glorious Cross.

V

In 1960 I did some lecturing on international and philosophical matters at Dartmouth College, and in 1961 I gave a course of lectures at the School of International Service of The American University in Washington, D.C., on philosophical issues in world relations. It was at various times during these two years, and independently of this lecturing activity, that the first drafts of these meditations were written. I must take this opportunity to express my gratitude and appreciation to the wonderful men I was privileged to know and work with and under in both of these institutions. The freedom and joy they afforded me made it possible for me to do lots of thinking and writing, of which this book is but the first fruit.

The occasions for writing these meditations were various invitations I had received and accepted to address several American religious bodies. The present book is based in part on some of these addresses. Other addresses, to Catholic and Orthodox audiences, and to other Protestant bodies, may be worked out into one or more additional books later. The selection for the present book is somewhat arbitrary, although a certain unity of spirit may be seen to blow through these seven chapters. The first version of Chapter I was delivered at a *Baptist* convention in Memphis, Tennessee, and part of this text was previously used before a *Methodist* convention in Washington, D.C., and in certain commencement addresses I gave in 1961; and these diverse organizations published the texts delivered before them, in part or in full, in their own publications. Chapter II is based on a text used for an *Episcopal* convention held in Detroit. Chapter III and V stem from addresses delivered before the meetings in 1960 and 1961 of the General Assembly of the United *Presbyterian* Church; and part of Chapter V as delivered appeared in *Presbyterian Life*. Chapter IV rests on a text used before a general convention of the *Congregational* Church held in Philadelphia; this Church distributed the original text among its membership in leaflet form, and the *Christian Century* published a version of it. Chapter VI originates in an address delivered at the National *Presbyterian* Church in Washington, D.C., and published in a changed form in the *Christian Century*. The original version of Chapter VII appeared in a private publication entitled *Unity is to fulfill, is to forgive*, put out for the Student Christian Movement in New England by 45 Garden Street Publications of Cambridge, Massachusetts. Thus Chapters II and III have not appeared before in any form in print. To these church bodies, to *Presbyterian Life*, to the *Christian Century* and to the publishers of *Unity is to fulfill, is to forgive*, I wish here to express my thanks for the use of material that first appeared, either in oral or written form, under their auspices. To Messrs. Wm. B. Eerdmans, Sr. and Jr., and their colleagues I wish also to express my gratitude for their unfailing courtesy, understanding and cooperation in seeing this book to print.

The present book is only *based* on these original drafts. In every case the original text was thoroughly gone over, and considerable changes, mostly in the form of additions and expansions, were introduced. The texts were rewritten expressly with this book in mind. Thus not only have Chapters II and III never been published before, but in every case new material was incorporated that was never even delivered before. And of course the text of this Foreword appears here for the first time.

VI

In writing a text to be delivered before an important church body, what is it that determines one's thought? How does the text develop, how does it come into being? Five factors are critically operative in the writing of such a text.

(1) As one writes, his prospective audience is before his mind all the time. He tries to imagine its state of existence and to argue with it. He is in fact *addressing* it. It suggests problems to him. He wants both to provoke and arouse it, and to call it to the depths. Thus the presiding presence of one's imagined audience determines the development of one's thought.

(2) He is addressing a *church* audience: therefore the Church comes into play. It is not feeling, or opinion, or thought, or some interesting theory or whim, or a passing issue of the day, or some silly political gossip, that he is primarily thinking of: it is the Church of Jesus Christ. No man can address a serious church audience without the being, the character and the tribulations of the Body of Christ somehow determining his thought. If he conceives his function only to cajole and amuse and entertain, he should never have accepted speaking in the first place.

(3) There is further his abiding personal relationship to Jesus Christ, his intimate knowledge of Him over the years, how much Christ has held him in the glorious bondage of His love and grace. It is because of this stable knowledge and relationship — *and only because of it* — that he *dares* speak, raise issues and challenge at all.

(4) Again, he is wrestling at the time with God and with the devil on a particular issue or temptation in his own life. This too fills his mind and colors his thought. No man knowing Jesus Christ and keeping His Church in mind can address a serious church audience in abstraction from the concrete spiritual struggles through which he is going at the time. He cannot but speak personally — how else does one live in the presence of Christ? If the theme is *occasioned* by the invitation to speak, its development is *dated* in the life of the speaker by the special suffering into which he is thrown at the time; or else the whole thing is unreal, academic and abstract.

(5) Then there is what I might call the general mood of the world. The world crisis poignantly haunts him, especially if he happens to have been thrown into the midst of it and therefore to have known something of its character. He must relate his audience, the Church, Jesus Christ and himself to the crisis. He cannot retire to a realm of eternal essences and think from outside the world, the way, for instance, the logicians and idealists do. He can only think and speak and act from within the world crisis in its actual, existing, most concrete character. This is the deepest thing about Jesus Christ: He came *to save the world* — this very world of space and time and history and decision and sin and suffering; God *became man* to save us men *in this world.* The development of the theme takes place with the world crisis, in its radical bearing upon our personal lives, as a determining background.

This is then how the theme suggests itself, develops and comes into being.

These factors determine every chapter in this book as

well as the book as a whole. Always there was the particular church audience, always the Church, always Jesus Christ, always the special trial of the moment, always the all-encompassing world crisis. The only unity to be found in this book therefore is the unity of these five factors bearing critically and jointly upon every point discussed. This is a transcendental and not an immanent unity; and as such it is the more genuine.

VII

What about error? What about departure from the truth? What about theological aberration and falsehood? This work, written somewhat freely and joyously, and more or less lyrically, cannot be altogether free from theological error. Now every writer has a secret audience whom he is really addressing. It could be a single man — *or woman.* It could be a special class of men — living *or dead.* But there is always a hidden audience whom the writer secretly has in mind and whom he seeks to please, an audience whose applause he wishes to merit. Determine who the secret audience of a writer is, determine *to whom he is really speaking,* and you can at once tell what he is likely to say and why he will say it. I ask the gentle reader to take the dozen or so writers he may have in mind and ask himself this question: *whom is this man trying to please?* It is a fascinating exercise. It could be that he is trying to please only "the public"; that then is pure commercialism and sophistry. It could be that he is trying to please "the powers that be"; that then is political shrewdness and calculation. It could be that he is trying to please his academic peers; that is the mark of high "scholarship." In the case of contemporary "technical philosophers," they form such exclusive "cliques" and "schools" that it is difficult to tell whom any of them is trying to please. One thing is obvious: they live in dreadful fright of each other; that is why they do not say much, lest they be immediately jumped upon and torn to pieces by the others who are waiting all the time precisely and only to do that; and that is why the utmost that some of them appear to be aiming at is *not to displease* those who belong to their own clique or school. But always, always there is a secret audience whom a writer frantically keeps in mind.

Who then is *my* secret audience? Whom do I secretly seek to please? Whom do I want to pass favorably on my performance? Whom do I wish to applaud me? Whose judgment and correction do I crave as to any theological error or distortion I may have committed?

I therefore say this: since I have no desire to make a "creative contribution" in the sacred field of theology, and since nothing can be farther from my mind than to "set up" or "start" anything new, even if I had the power to do so, I recant in advance every statement or implication in this book — and consider it absolutely null and void — that is at variance with Holy Scripture, or the teachings of the Fathers, or the determinations of the Councils, or the tradition of the Saints, or the doctrines of the great Doctors, especially Augustine and Chrysostom, or the beliefs and practices of the One, Holy, Catholic and Apostolic Church in which I believe and to which I belong, or that a person like Teresa of Avila or Dostoyevski would strongly object to.

May, 1962 —CHARLES MALIK
Chevy Chase, Maryland

CHAPTER I

THE SPIRITUAL RESPONSE TO THE CRISIS

I

There are three unpardonable sins today: to be flippant or superficial in the analysis of the world situation; to live and act as though halfhearted measures would avail; and to lack the moral courage to rise to the historic occasion. To err intellectually, to be sloppy and slothful in one's mode of living, and, for any reason, to play the coward — these can easily doom Western civilization, either through some sudden world cataclysm, or through the slow decay and death that come from the paralysis of fear.

Everybody has a role to play. Government, business, labour, the press, the university, the churches — every agency and every person must respond, each in his own way and each within the limits of his competence.

The matter of competence is most important, for to ask, as some people do, What is the Church doing, or what is the university doing?, and to have in mind when one asks this question that the Church or the university is not doing, for example, what the press or the government is doing, and therefore is doing nothing, is most irresponsible. Similarly, to expect the government or those in authority to preach forgiveness and love and to neglect the security and well-being of the state is to expect the government to be a church. This does not mean that the Church "neglects" the security and well-being of the state; the Church is profoundly "interested" in these things; but the securing of them is not its primary responsibility, any more than that the changing of the hearts of men to love and to forgive one another is the primary responsibility of the state. A not inconsiderable number of most harmful fallacies arise because people arrogate to themselves what does not properly fall within their competence: the clergyman talks as though he were responsible for deciding the political fate of his country; or as though the school should perform the function of the Church; or as though the fate of civilization is wholly determined by his feeling or his prayer. Distribution of competence and division of responsibility is of the essence of all civilized existence.

II

The situation resolves itself into four interacting dimensions: (1) there is the challenge of international Communism; (2) there is the challenge of the rising nations and peoples; (3) there are serious internal challenges and problems in the West itself; and (4) there is the formidable challenge of the technological revolution.

The character of the Communist challenge consists, first, in a conception of matter, man, society, history, government, and the supreme being radically different from and radically opposite to anything you and I and your ancestors and mine have known for the last four thousand years; second, in the existence of a superbly organized political party, the Marxist-Leninist Communist Party, with an absolutely dedicated membership all over the world of about forty million people, actively working day and night in every country to bring every people on earth under the bondage of this philosophy of existence; third, in the fact that this Party uses every conceivable means — war, revolution, subversion, infiltration, propaganda, intimidation, dictatorship, manipulation of the masses, smear tactics, character assassination, exciting the basest instincts in man, playing up differences and grievances between nations and peoples and races and classes —· to attain its unalterable end of world domination; fourth, in the fact that this world revolutionary thrust is backed by one of the most powerful military establishments in the world — in fact some people think it is already the most powerful military force; and fifth, in the fact that this world revolutionary force, notwithstanding the innumerable ups and downs it went through during the last forty-five years, has always in the end managed to come out triumphant, and has succeeded in extending and consolidating its iron hold upon at least a third of the human race.

The rising peoples ask in effect four questions: (1) Who can help us best to enjoy our basic human rights? (2) What measures and methods can enable us to progress fast enough to meet our old as well as our rising needs? (3) Who can give us the warmth and security of his fellowship without exploiting us and without infringing upon our freedom and self-respect? (4) What is the place of our culture, our interpretation of things, in relation to other cultures and other points of view? The rising peoples have every right to ask these questions and every right to expect to receive an answer to them.

III

Concerning the internal problems of the West I might mention that there is such an extraordinary multiplicity of stimuli that the mind is dangerously distracted. Life in many instances appears to have lost its original simplicity. There are too many techniques and there is not enough unity of spirit. Wealth has greatly increased, bringing in its trail both opportunities for high attainment on a large scale, and opportunities for indulgence and softness of living. Moral standards are not as firm and certain as according to the deepest tradition of the West they should be. There are divisions among the ranks of the Western powers, divisions which often impair the effectiveness of the Western impact upon the rest of the world. The classical Western values of freedom, personality, excellence, rank, objective truth, faith in God, and the primacy of the spirit, are subverted both by Communist infiltration from without and by doubt and criticism by some of the best Western minds from within. In many identifiable instances one is not sure that what is believed differs ultimately much from Communist ideals, except perhaps in modality and degree. Secularism, socialism and atheism are rampant, and while the actual living God is not militantly and openly combated, He is at best politely tolerated. The notion that man possesses an immortal soul absolutely responsible to its creator is in complete decay. Fundamental faith in God making a creative difference to the whole tone and orientation of existence is not in dazzling evidence. Endless techniques, infinite cleverness, but the dimension of "the beyond," "the above," is missing. And I fear the full magnitude of the Communist and anti-Western challenge is not adequately understood and feared.

The challenge of the technological revolution is simply that the scientists have unleashed such tremendous elemental forces that, while through folly these forces can easily destroy mankind, through wisdom and the spirit of God they can lift all men onto a bright new plane of happiness, peace, and wonder.

The world today, then, is a field of interaction between the West and its heretical offshoot, Communism, and between these two and the old-new peoples of Asia and Africa, and between all three and that strange spark in man which we call science and theory and which, in man's self-consciousness of it and his discovery of the methods of training and perfecting it, goes back to the ancient Greeks.

IV

This is a total challenge, and anything short of a total response to it is a fraud.

To begin with, the Communist challenge must be seriously taken for what it is: a radical transvaluation of all hitherto tested and received values. It does not take an interview of eight hours with Khrushchev to discover its nature: the thing is fully and unambiguously explained in their classical writings. While it is encouraging to note that in recent years there has been a distinct enhancement in the understanding of the real character of Communism, still there are many influential people who preach, or who at least are taken by, "peaceful coexistence," and who appear to be prepared to settle for peace at almost any price or for what is falsely called "mutual accommodation," where accommodation turns out upon analysis to come only from one side. Having regard to the concrete forces at work, it is possible — although God forbid! — that this awakening has come too late.

The Communists teach and believe that the Communist proletarian revolution culminating everywhere in the dictatorship of the proletariat is the inevitable wave of the future. They work day and night to make it so. Nothing that happened during the last forty years has proved them wrong. Their march may have been slowed here and there and they may have been forced to zigzag in endless ways and to alter their timetable practically every other year, but they have not been dislodged one inch from where they have been really entrenched. Thus it is most important that at least one significant dislodging be produced to invalidate Communist historical determinism. It is not enough to prevent them from reaching this or that place, although even this containing attempt has not been altogether successful, as witness their amazing victories in recent years in Asia, Africa and Latin America; it is necessary to uproot them from where they have actually taken root. Otherwise history will remain on their side, and history is the most potent of teachers. Nor is it enough to proclaim piously that freedom shall win; it is necessary to plan and work in order to produce one significant instance in which it has actually won against Communism.

Surely every conceivable weapon should be employed in self-defense — military, political, diplomatic, economic, psychological. Now there are limits to self-defense, because mere self-defense could become self-defeating, and because, precisely in self-defense, one must at times pass to the offensive. What concerns us most here is the moral and spiritual weapon. And here too this dialectic of the defense and the offense is most apparent. Morally and spiritually the Communists put you and me on the defensive; they make us feel guilty, and we supinely accept the terms of their debate. They talk in terms of "capitalism," "imperialism," "colonialism," "monopolies," "profits," "exploitation," "means of production," — all purely economic, purely materialistic terms. And in answering them usually all we say is that the exploiting capitalism of the nineteenth century no longer exists, imperialism has been liquidated, monopolies are now owned by the people, and as to profits, everybody now shares in them. There is about this response a pathetic air of apology, a ring of feebleness, a sickly note of timidity. We answer the Communists as though they were the accusers and we the accused; we accept their universe of discourse; we stupidly let ourselves be drawn into their materialistic dialectic.

This will not do. They should be answered, not apologetically, not on a materialistic basis, but in human, moral, and spiritual terms.

V

Those who really wish to pass to the offensive morally and spiritually must turn to the Communists and say:

What about freedom of thought and inquiry in your realm? Can people seek the truth really freely? Can they really dissent? Can they really question your fundamental assumptions?

What about human rights and fundamental freedoms? Which of these rights are really enjoyed by your people?

What about freedom of conscience and religion? Do

you Communists go to church? Do you fall on your knees and pray? And why do you persecute those who do?

Is there any free criticism of the government in your realm? Have your people ever been given a genuine free political choice?

What about your iron dictatorship? What about your police state?

What about the minority rule under which all Communist states languish?

What about the methods of subversion all over the world in which every dark trick of deceit and destruction is used?

What about the camps of forced labor?

It is only as the total arsenal of political, moral and spiritual values are thus brought to bear that there is any hope of winning in this tremendous struggle. Naturally, if you do not believe that a mortal struggle is already upon us, you will not care to struggle at all. Naturally, if you do not believe in the primacy of these political, personal, moral and spiritual values, you will not bring them up at all. Naturally, if you are already converted to the materialistic standpoint of your opponents, you will argue with them only in terms of the gross national product, of raising the standard of living, of the rate of growth of the productivity of the nation, of social and economic justice, and of economic security and social benefits. The Communists love to confine you within that round of ideas. But the historic struggle in which we are engaged today is primarily moral, personal and spiritual, and to miss or minimize that dimension of the struggle is already to have been vanquished by those who believe that the moral, personal and spiritual is nothing but the "secretion" of matter and economics.

The greatest weakness of Western strategy is its relative neglect of the intellectual and spiritual dimension. This is strange, because intellectual, moral and spiritual matters are the greatest point of strength in the Western arsenal. While it is most essential that in arms and armaments, in scientific and technological inventiveness, and in the flooding of the world with materials goods, the Communists should not be allowed to gain and maintain an edge, still it is primarily in the realm of the mind, the realm of the spirit and its wonderful grace, the realm of human and moral valuation, that the West has a tremendous advantage. It all depends then on whether there are still strong enough forces in the West who passionately believe in and vigorously and constantly work for and boldly and singlemindedly proclaim the original primacy of the mind and spirit.

VI

The questions which the rising peoples ask deserve every respect and they should certainly be answered; and I assure you I am no idealist who believes that their material and social needs can be met just by ideas lofty and hopes pious and high. Now and for a number of years to come it is possible, with vision and determination, to beat the Communists in helping the less developed peoples economically and materially. Peaceful competition in this realm should not frighten the West at all: its resources, properly marshaled and coordinated, are for many years to come — and it would be the fault of the West if they did not remain so almost indefinitely — more than a match for anything the Communists can put forth in any open and fair competition. But here again economic assistance is not enough: the soul and heart of these people must also be reached.

How they may develop, in freedom, the healthy sense of absolute equality and respect; how they may be convinced that their dignity is sacrosanct; how to extend to them the hand of fellowship without encroaching on their freedom and independence; how to make them feel, without spoiling or pampering them, that they have genuine native values which they should preserve and of which they may be proud; how to pass on to them the canons of a higher critique of their own existence, past and present, without casting them into the slough of despair; how to accept with grace and humility and gratitude the constructive role which they can play in international affairs, on the basis of genuineness and truth, and not of sentimentality and mutual bluff; how to help them attain the national security and social vigor that they so constantly dream of and so desperately strive after, without either their lapsing back into a status of dependency or their becoming chauvinistic — all this requires much more than the knowledge of the technicians and the good will of the well-intentioned: all this is going to tax the wisdom and imagination and foresight and spiritual depth of the highest thinkers and statesmen of the West.

VII

The crisis is certainly military, for on the question, who has the greater military might — the Communist world or the free world?, everything in a sense depends. If the balance of power has decisively tipped in one direction, then the fate of the other side is already sealed, and there is left only the modality of its surrender or the ritual of its burial. I do not believe the balance has tipped against freedom; what is possible is that there is a most uneasy equilibrium, a sort of stalemate; but with one fundamental breakthrough in the technological revolution the balance could become decisively favorable or decisively adverse. This military aspect of the crisis, the generals and technicians are alone competent to gauge and to handle, and on their wise ensuring that a favorable balance is maintained and augmented, everything in the end depends.

The crisis is certainly political, for on the question, which system is more in accordance with nature and therefore more true — the totalitarian system or the free system?, everything in a sense depends. There is no doubt that the free system which respects the dignity and rights of man is the more true and more enduring. The free world must therefore fearlessly expose the falsity of totalitarianism and prevent it from imposing itself by force upon the artless and naive. For evil and falsehood can for a time overtake and destroy the good. This political aspect of the crisis, the politicians and the statesmen are alone competent to gauge and to handle, and on their energy and daring in defending and extending the domain of freedom and man, everything in the end depends.

The crisis is certainly economic, for on the question, which system is more productive and more just — the Communist system or the system of responsible freedom?, everything in a sense depends. None of the Communist countries has as yet caught up or is in sight of catching up with the standard of living of the free. And every fault or flaw in the free system can be freely corrected without paying the awful price of freedom smothered and dignity trodden under foot. This economic aspect of the crisis, the economists, the industrialists and the businessmen are alone competent to gauge and to handle, and on their actually demonstrating that responsible free economy could produce more abundantly and distribute more justly without unduly regimenting the creative energies of man, everything in the end depends.

The crisis is certainly scientific, for on the question, which side is going to see more deeply into the secrets of nature and to harness more effectively her forces — the Communist side or the free side?, everything in a sense depends. Never was competition in theory and research more intense and more determinant of the destiny of whole nations and whole cultures than it is today. The concentration of theoretical talent and facilities for research in the free world far outweighs anything that the Communist world can boast of. Therefore the free world would have only its negligence and its lack of co-ordination to blame if the Communist world should get ahead of it in the foreseeable future in this all-important realm. This scientific aspect of the crisis, the scientists and theorists are alone competent to gauge and to handle, and on their ensuring, with the assistance of the statesmen and politicians, that research and theory are always vigorously pursued by an ever expanding army of adequately trained men who are absolutely happy in their living and working conditions, everything in the end depends.

The crisis is certainly intellectual, for on the question, which commands a truer and a deeper philosophy — the realm of Marx and Lenin or the realm of Plato and Aristotle?, everything in a sense depends. What is at stake here is man: his nature, his origin, his destiny, his understanding of himself. Is he a machine? Is he an animal with blind natural impulses and nothing more? Is he a mere cog in the wheel of the state? Is he a mechanical product of his social conditions? Or is he created by God after His own likeness and image, and therefore endowed with reason, with inherent dignity and with an immortal soul? The sordid materialism of Marx has, alas, infected the West, but the West remains the integral depository of the deepest intellectual vision ever disclosed to man. This intellectual aspect of the crisis, the thinkers and philosophers are alone competent to gauge and to handle, and on their re-asserting the original potency of mind and reason, as an inalienable part of the Western heritage, everything in the end depends.

VIII

The crisis breaks up into so many aspects, all of which are absolutely real, and all with competent men to appreciate and do something about. But in its deepest dimension the crisis is spiritual. It has to do with God, with how much men still acknowledge Him and how much they still obey Him. Let God be known and loved, and the military requirements, the political problems, the economic needs, the scientific issues, and the vision of the intellect, will all take care of themselves. On the crisis of God every other crisis depends.

And so I ask, what may the churches do? What is their specific role in the total response? And the first thing is to recognize that, while their role is very important, still it is very limited. They cannot take responsibility for military or political or economic or scientific or intellectual decisions. They know precious little about these matters, and therefore they cannot presume to advise on them. These five fields — the military, the political, the economic, the scientific and the intellectual — simply fall outside the competence of the churches. The utmost that can be hoped for here is that those who do take responsibility for these decisions are themselves Christians, impregnated with the mind of Christ, with all the wonderful illumination and sense of responsibility that that mind provides. But the churches as such have quite a different sphere of competence.

In the prevailing climate of materialism, secularism and religious indifference they certainly are called to new heroic effort. They must keep the flame of the creative spirit burning. Let them attend to this properly, and everything else will follow. And the churches alone can fire the spirit to new heights of vision, daring and being. They alone can cause men to seek first the kingdom of God and His righteousness, and all else then will be added unto them.

The Church does three things: she convicts us all of our sin and thus she keeps us all in the presence and fear of God; she wields the weapons of the spirit in the face of all that is spiritually neutral and all this is anti-truth, anti-being, and anti-Christ; and, regardless of what happens in the world and to the world, she remains absolutely faithful to Jesus Christ. In these three realms the Church is absolutely supreme — to instill the fear of God, to fight the devil, and to witness to Jesus Christ. Nothing and nobody can take her place here, and therefore if she busies herself with other matters, the most important things will be left unattended to and undone.

The Church convicts us of our sin as she lifts the Cross above every principality and every power. Then we realize how lustful we have been; how proud, how unrepentant; how rebellious, how disobedient, how grasping and selfish, how untrusting; then we see the hold of sin and the devil on our own life. Perhaps then we will fall on our knees; perhaps we will be shattered and humbled; perhaps we will pray. Only through repentance, penance and prayer — the most ardent prayer we can possibly call forth — can God help us and can we help in saving the world. And the help and salvation of God in Jesus Christ is the utmost joy and certainty and power we can think of; it is exactly what is called life eternal.

The Church wields the weapons of the spirit in the face of untruth and anti-truth by firmly maintaining the right order of value, by declaring that the Spirit comes first and everything else second, by meekly and gently affirming that God is the Creator, Christ the Redeemer and the Holy Ghost the Giver of Life and the guide into all truth. But the weapons of the spirit cannot be wielded with efficacy in the face of untruth and anti-truth except if the scandal of disunity is overcome. Untruth and anti-truth enjoy a field day when they see the Church splintered and divided. There is therefore much to repent of and much to pray for, not only in our own individual lives, but in and for the corporate life of the Body of Christ.

The Church remains faithful to Jesus Christ by not tying her fate to the fate of systems and governments and orders and cultures and civilizations. The Church is neither Western nor Eastern; she is neither Aryan nor Slav; she is neither Anglo-Saxon nor Latin; she is neither capitalist nor proletarian; she is neither white nor colored;

she is neither European nor Asian nor African nor American: she is the Church of Jesus Christ by whose "Spirit are we all baptized into one body, whether we be Jews or Gentiles, whether we be bond or free" (I Corinthians 12:13). In the present terrific clash of culture and ideology I do not know what God is holding in store for us all. I do not know what shall befall this or that system, this or that order, this or that point of view. While defending and identifying herself with truth wherever she finds it, the Church should above all maintain her independence of all worldly fortunes and all the kingdoms of the world. The Church has a separate realm of her own, the most wonderful realm that there is, a realm which even the gates of hell shall not prevail against. Let the Church therefore remain faithful to the kingdom of God and His Christ. If — God forbid! — the world and its kingdoms should go up in smoke, let at least the name of Christ remain above every name and let the Cross shine above every symbol. In the world the Church can only wield the weapons of the spirit in all purity; she can only wield them helplessly, namely, with the naked help of the Cross; and having thus wielded them, she humbly trusts the issue to God. The issue is always in His hands.

CHAPTER II

THE CHURCH AND THE INTERNATIONAL ORDER

I

One cannot sit back and philosophize about such themes as "The Church and the International Order." If one does that, then one is only expressing his point of view, and I hate expressing — I hate even thinking of — my point of view when it comes to such fundamental matters. Either there is a God who is living and who is absolutely there, and therefore whose point of view we should first and foremost seek, or we are hopelessly lost in the darkness of our private points of view which never cease to contradict themselves and one another. There is a radical difference between one who gloats over his ideas, even his ideas of God, and one who seeks to find out if God Himself has spoken. The latter may indeed mistake the word of the devil for the word of God, but he is at least seeking a voice speaking from beyond. And if his heart is pure, he can recognize which is the voice of God and which the voice of the devil. For in these matters there is no joke, in these matters the search can never be in vain: for God is certainly "a rewarder of them that diligently seek him" (Hebrews 11:6). "I have

17

not spoken in secret, in a dark place of the earth: I said not unto the seed of Jacob, Seek ye me in vain: I the Lord speak righteousness, I declare things that are right" (Isaiah 45:19). God speaks clearly through His word in Holy Scripture, through the established doctrine, tradition and life of the Church, including above all the Sacraments, and through the communion of saints. It follows that whatever I say on our present theme that is at variance with the Bible or the teaching or tradition or life of the Church or the wonderful witness of the saints, is *ipso facto* null and void: I recant it in advance. For who can say that the international order exists and moves outside the grasp and providence of almighty God?

II

When we speak of "The Church and the International Order" the first temptation, especially in times of great crisis, is to imagine that the Church is the mere servant of the nations; that she should spend all her time seeking how she might be "used" by them; that she exists just to worry about their affairs, to intervene in their squabbles, to seek to prevent them from falling out with one another, and in general to promote what is called the "cause of peace." This is a sentimental and unauthentic interpretation of the role of the Church, and nothing is more dismaying these days — when world issues are so much on the mind of everybody — than the ease with which some of those who have known the grace and power and salvation of Christ so placidly fall into this temptation. For there is no evidence, either in the Bible or in the tradition or in the witness of the saints, that this is the function of the Church. The Church cannot compromise her integrity by assuming responsibility for the fortunes or misfortunes of the world. Let that responsibility be borne solely by the princes of the world who decide its fate. Politics and world affairs belong primarily to politicians; salvation and the ultimate affairs of the soul belong exclusively to the Church.

When we pray, as our Lord taught us, "thy will be done on earth as it is in heaven," the meaning can never be that, just because there is perfect peace in heaven, God's will is that there should be perfect peace on earth under any conditions. For what about human sin and human apostasy? What about the devil who is certainly rampant on earth but is not permitted to come anywhere near heaven? Can God's will be to reward even sin and the devil with peace and quiet and contentment? Wouldn't that contradict every word in the Psalms? May not God's will be precisely that the doers of evil, the haters of God and Christ, the lovers of the devil and his works, the worshipers of all that is spiteful and negative and dark, the unforgiving, the revengeful, the scornful, the cynics, the envious, the covetous, the perpetually contradicting, the blaspheming against all that is holy and pure, should suffer here on earth even if that should entail also the suffering of the righteous and good? There is no evidence whatsoever that "peace at any price" is part of the will of God on earth.

"Vengeance is mine; I will repay, saith the Lord" (Romans 12:19; Deuteronomy 32:35; Psalm 94:1; Hebrews 10:30) means five things: (1) that we should always forgive and never seek revenge, for if we sought revenge we would be usurping the place of God; (2) that because the world is in His hands, vengeance belongs to God alone, and therefore, since He is just, we should expect Him to execute

it, certainly in the world to come, but perhaps also even
in this world; (3) that when the innocent do suffer together with the guilty on earth, it is principally due to
the wisdom and justice of God which often we may
not discern, but it is also a token of the solidarity of
the human race which man, in his stupidity and sin,
has divided by a thousand partitions; (4) that if we
suffer in the day of vengeance, even if we had always
forgiven, even if we never sought revenge but always
left the act of retribution to God Himself, it could very
well be that we were not as innocent and pure and spotless
as we thought we were; and (5) that should God in His
inscrutable goodness have mercy on sinners — as He as-
suredly does when He pleases, and we simply do not understand it — and forgive their transgression and impute no
iniquity unto them (Psalm 32:1-2), then far from mur-
muring and arguing with Him, we should beware lest our
eye be evil because He is good (Matthew 20:11-15).
"Vengeance is mine, saith the Lord" means that we should
always fear His vengeance and always be on our knees
seeking His forgiveness and always trust and marvel at
His infinite mercy.

III

It follows that international disorder and war should
not surprise the Church. She will do nothing to cause
them; she will never incite the nations to war or the
peoples to disorder; on the contrary, she will always
ardently pray and work for peace and order; she will always
exhort the nations to keep the peace; she will warn them
with the utmost solicitation against resorting to war; but
she will always also pray, first and last, that God's will
be done, a will that is certainly above everything, in-

cluding the nations and the so-called "peace" that they willfully forge among themselves, a peace so different and so distant from the peace of God which passeth all understanding (Philippians 4:7).

It follows also that the Church understands perfectly how God can permit war. And when He does — as again and again He has throughout history — without her having had anything to do with it, and despite her prayers and supplications, she does not on that account cease to believe in His righteousness and His love, nor does she forthwith flee into the deistic notion that anything on earth, including war, takes place outside his knowledge or against His will. On the contrary, in peace or in war, and in war more than in peace, she always cries with Paul, "let God be true, but every man a liar" (Romans 3:4); and it is an integral part of her faith to understand and interpret everything in such a way that, whether in peace or in war, and in war more than in peace, God might be justified and might overcome when He is judged (*ibid.*).

In peace or in war the Church has her hands full, and in war perhaps even more than in peace. For not only does she suffer with the suffering in war, but while in peace she cannot work for war, in war she must on top of her ordinary duties of bringing God to man and man to God also work for peace.

IV

But *to be herself* it is her primary business that the Church, war or no war, can never abdicate and must always be about, to wit, to confess God the Creator,

Jesus Christ the only-begotten Son of God, and the Holy Ghost the Lord and Giver of Life.

What does this primary task mean, this business of the Church, this confession which is so total, so serious, so independent, so time-consuming, so preoccupying, that in order to dedicate her whole life to it the Church must live in complete detachment from the affairs of the world — from its wars and revolutions, its orders and disorders, its systems and its governments — even if the world should go up in smoke, a detachment that appears so selfish and hardhearted and that is therefore so irksome and annoying to the world that the Church has suffered endless misunderstandings and persecutions as a result?

The Church's business is to remain absolutely faithful to what she has received. She is to guard and keep the divine mysteries that have been entrusted to her. She is to administer the Sacraments, doubting nothing, and with a mind absolutely upright and correct. She is to preserve, to expound and to hand down the Word of God.

Faithful in her task, the Church convicts us men of our sin and proclaims to us God's forgiveness in Jesus Christ on the Cross. She provides the faithful with opportunities for worship, prayer, penance and the fellowship of the Holy Ghost.

Faithful in her teaching, the Church always confesses the victory of Jesus Christ over the world and the devil, a victory always freely available to those who love and believe in Him. In the smallest of her words and in the simplest of her deeds, she lives wholly by faith, and she transmits this power of faith to those who really want to live.

In the Church the soul feasts on the wonderful words

and stories and events of the Gospel, words that were said and stories that were told and events that took place, it is true humbly and obscurely in Palestine, but certainly not in some dark prehistoric time, but in the full blaze of history, under Tiberius and Augustus, events that, so far as the total span of history is concerned, I might almost say happened only yesterday.

The impact of this story, faithfully and humbly told, and lovingly pondered, is to show that in Jesus Christ God is reconciling miserable man to Himself. This the Church demonstrates daily in the innumerable instances of sinners, truly repenting and therefore truly forgiven, being restored in their complete oneness with God — their innocence, their purity, their transparency, their freedom, returning exactly to what they were before their fall, but with the added infinitely creative joy that comes from the assured knowledge that they have been forgiven, and forgiven indeed not by man, but by God.

Faithful in her life and ministry, the Church maintains and daily augments a fountainhead of grace and contemplation. When the soul really drinks from this fountainhead, or even when it approaches it, heaven literally opens before it. And in the divine liturgy the soul receives its most wonderful schooling. There is an absolute assurance of God, a most hopeful wrestling with the powers of darkness, a certainty that the love of God in Jesus Christ understands all and overcomes all. But above all, it is the gift of tears, cleansing the heart, reviving the soul, releasing the spirit, for which the believer is most thankful in the Holy Ghost.

In the way she meets and overcomes her trials; in the wonder of her unbroken history; in the incredible communion of saints whereby when we read Paul or Augustine they speak to our inmost soul; in the fellowship of the Holy Ghost whereby the faithful, in heaven and on earth, in the present and throughout all history, suffer together, hold together, stand together, praise God together, and feel one another's enriching and sustaining presence; in the consolation of the Holy Ghost which opens the mind, confirms the faith and reveals the truth marvelously; and in the numerous acts and institutions of mercy and charity which she sponsors and supports: in this performance of her confession the Church proves her independent origin and bears witness to a destiny quite separate from the world.

"Ye are the salt of the earth . . . . Ye are the light of the world" (Matthew 5:13, 14) — He did not say of one nation or one people, or of twenty nations or twenty peoples, but of the whole inhabited world!

And so, if all this concrete content is what the Church's confession and business is about, what more do the nations want, even for their internal order, even for their order among themselves, even for peace?

V

Why have I set forth this essential business of the Church before a gathering of Bishops and Clergy who know infinitely more about it than I do? I have done so for two reasons: (a) to point out that this business of the Church is the most important thing in the world, and that therefore there is no room for the Church to envy the statesmen or politicians or to seek to take their place in the determination of events; and (b) to suggest that, in her genuine interest in the international order, the Church can speak, not from the point of view of this or that nation, or this or that culture, or this or that system, but only from the point of view of Jesus Christ who is her living Head and of whom she is the living Body. If as it were I hailed here before you *from the nations,* and if you wished to know what the nations wanted from the Church — whether or not they knew what they wanted — then what I am saying is only that the nations expect the Church *to be the Church.*

From the nations the Church expects three things. First, she asks for the freedom to preach the Gospel in every land and to every people and culture. Of course she can never impose her will, but, knowing her rights under God, neither can she relent in her demand that she be granted the freedom *to be the Church* everywhere, even if she should suffer many martyrdoms as a result. And mysterious doors will be opened to her even when the world in its stupidity closes them before her face.

Second, she insists on natural principles of justice, truth, the common good, the dignity of man, and that man can never be treated as a means only. She must make absolutely plain that these principles are not accidental or arbitrary, nor are they granted as a favour by the state, so that they might be withdrawn or tampered with at will, but they spring from the nature of things, and ultimately from the mind of God Himself.

Third, she insists that diverse nations, peoples and cultures, being all "made of one blood . . . for to dwell on all the face of the earth" (Acts 17:26), have each a worth of its own, so that they are entitled by nature to a life of dignity and independence, always under conditions of mutual respect and with due regard for the common good.

Beyond these three fundamental demands the Church cannot go without courting endless risks. And if she feels she must go beyond them on this or that specific issue, she must first make absolutely sure that she knows all the facts before she commits herself. I have read pronouncements by churchmen and resolutions by Church bodies on Communist China and the United Nations, on the revision of the United Nations Charter, on so-called "peaceful coexistence," on disarmament, on banning atomic tests, on this or that system of government or type of economy, and on so-called "peace" — and I mention these seven instances only because I know a little about them — I say I have read pronouncements and resolutions on these matters that only prove that those who made them were either tendentious or did not know all the facts. And neither naiveté nor tendentiousness becomes the Church.

VI

This is as far as the Church can go in her demands *from* the nations. But on top of her *being the Church,* she can do much *for* the nations.

She can rejoice that peoples and nations are becoming free all over the world, and she can actively hope that this movement will not be confined to one part of the world only.

In the present general collapse of morals, the Church can instil absolute moral standards among her people, to the end that the nations may depend on a citizenry that believes in and practices integrity, honesty, truthfulness, clean living, personal responsibility, courage in the face of adversity, and the heroic life.

The Church can rejoice if there are Christians in positions of high authority, and she can support and pray for them, although she can never be responsible for their decisions and their views; and whatever the ups and downs they go through in their life, they should be made to feel that the Church is always there to love them, understand them, replenish their soul, and give them the deepest fellowship.

Since there is no reason whatsoever why the affairs of the nations should be helplessly left to men who do not love Christ and who do not know His mind, the Church can urge her fold to see to it that Christians be sent and kept in positions of great responsibility.

You have no idea how much lonely people in such positions value the assurance that, while they alone are responsible for their decisions, the Church nevertheless is daily remembering them in her prayers before the altar of almighty God.

While working and witnessing under any conditions, and while believing that God can turn any evil to His glory, the Church nevertheless can examine any economic, social or political order in the light of the mind of Christ.

Since what matters about peace is not its form but its content, the Church can always scrutinize the character of peace as to whether it is just, whether it promotes the dignity of man, and whether under its aegis the rights of God are respected; but she can never be responsible either for confirming or for upsetting whatever international peace there is.

The Church can rejoice that Jesus Christ is not left without witnesses in Russia today, and seeing in this fact, far above any present-day political or economic differences, a real hope for reconciliation in God's own time, she can seek to strengthen to the utmost the bond of fellowship with these great heroes of the spirit.

The Church can rejoice that the Gospel has been preached to the uttermost ends of the earth, and through the eye of faith she can see this as one of the greatest facts of this age, determining perhaps every other fact.

The Church may never derive God from the world and its manifold cultures and civilizations; on the contrary, she should study to see how everything good and stable in every culture and civilization ultimately derives from Him.

The Church can never exclude the possibility that we may be today at the end of history when our Lord Himself is returning, and that therefore all the present sufferings and the certain sufferings to come may only be attendant upon His sending forth His angels to "gather out of his kingdom all things that offend, and them which do iniquity" (Matthew 13:41).

In loving Christ and living Christ, the Church will accept the judgment of God and be thankful, even if that judgment should mean the end of the world.

The greatest service that the Church, in *being the Church,* can render in and for the international order is to try to bring about an effective spiritual unity among all those who have been baptized in the name of the Father, of the Son and of the Holy Ghost. I believe conditions today are propitious for such a unity. I also believe that special responsibility devolves on the churches that stress the episcopal principle. If it should be God's will that unity come about in our time, then every problem in the international order would be miraculously transformed. Let us all therefore "lift up the hands which hang down, and the feeble knees" (Hebrews 12:12), and pray and work for this unity. The Holy Ghost may still surprise the most skeptical among us with His wonder-working power. The deepest prayer that any man can utter is this: "May I never be found guilty of resisting the Holy Ghost."

CHAPTER III

GO YE AND PREACH THE GOSPEL

I

The Church of Jesus Christ is a fighting Church. When she ceases to fight, she is on the way to ceasing to exist. Firm in her faith and foundation, she has nevertheless always faced a hostile world. She faces a hostile world today. "I send you forth as sheep in the midst of wolves . . . . And ye shall be hated of all men for my name's sake" (Matthew 10:16, 22). Wolves hating the very name of Jesus Christ are as rampant and prowling today as in the days of our Lord.

Bishops, priests, and ministers of the Word, filled with the Gospel and wrestling with their immediate situation, never tire of pointing out in their sermons all over the world that there are foxes like Herod living today; there are Pilates in our midst who timidly and calculatingly wash their hands of Christ; there are Agrippas who are almost persuaded; there are Pharisees and hypocrites like unto whited sepulchres; there are Sadducees who have no thought of the life to come; there are adulterers who nevertheless wash the feet of Christ with their tears; there are adulteresses who wipe His feet with their hair; there are Marthas who are busy with all sorts of things, save the most needful and most important; there are fathers who sincerely cry out, "I believe; help thou mine unbelief" (Mark 9:24); there are wonderful young men who go away sorrowful because they are not prepared to part with their possessions, a piffle of a price compared to what they will receive in return; there are Judases who betray their friends — and for what?: for silly material advantages — only to wake up later on and hang themselves; there are Barnabases who suddenly for some reason drop out of the picture altogether; there are Sauls, hating and threatening and killing, who nevertheless in God's own time suddenly become wonderful instruments of Christ; there are Peters, ignorant, simple, fickle, impulsive, but basically with a heart of gold, on whom heaven can build its house on earth, far better and far more securely than on the greatest philosophers; there are people, good people, to whom the Cross of Christ is a stumblingblock and a scandal, who have no notion and want to have no notion of what it is all about; and of course there are Athenians who would love to hear some new gossip or conjecture — such as what is happening in Geneva or Washington, or what is the chance of overthrowing Castro, or whether the missile gap will be closed or has been closed or had ever existed — but when it comes to Christ and His resurrection, they call that babbling and they defer hearing further about it until a future time.

II

In all these situations, the Church faces today the same types of men, the same opposing forces, the same recalcitrance, as she did when God first walked on earth. The world is by no means converted, and those who love

Christ today must fight against the forces of darkness with all their strength, as it was ever their lot in the past to do.

I ask: What is the *human joy* of the Gospel? The human joy of the Gospel is that it is as relevant to our situation today as to any situation in the past, and that it is *inconceivable* that it will not be equally relevant to any situation in the future. Let those who speak of human progress tell us then where is that progress when it comes to the relevance of the Gospel of Jesus Christ. It is this eternal timeliness of the Gospel that infuses the heart of the Christian with the deepest human joy. He knows that he is not here dealing with the fashion of the world: he knows that this is the unchanging character of God. And what an infinite rejoicing seizes him when he realizes that his reactions to this wonderful story are identical with the reactions of every Christian throughout history. He thus enters into the unutterable communion of saints.

For the Gospel pierces our heart, convicts our soul, exposes our motives, reveals our secret desires, analyzes our character, brings us up smack against a wall before which we must take a stand, sorts us all out into sheep and goats and all sorts of intermediate beasts, makes us all supremely uneasy, and always keeps us in the glow of the hope of the mercy of God. No man is not immediately and totally judged by the Gospel. And when the Christian realizes that here therefore is an instrument that confronts man eternally, that confronts essential human nature from the beginning to the end of time, with its eternal judge, namely, with the one true God, who is the same yesterday, today, and forever, he is plunged into utter amazement, and he becomes simply thankful. The Gospel arouses, provokes, stings, judges, and at the same time it heals; it cannot heal without first stinging; and it is this stinging-healing instrument which is the only weapon with which the Church faces and fights a hostile world.

And not only so. Do you think that the heresies which the Church fought and refuted in the past have been once and for all completely silenced? Do you think there are no more Christian Jews who want Christ only to themselves; no more Manichees, no more Pelagians, no more Gnostics, no more Donatists, no more Arians, no more Nestorians, no more Monothelites, no more Albigensians? If you think so, then you do not know human nature, nor certainly do you know the modern world. Nothing is more fascinating than to be able to identify the same old demons of heresy and disruption in the political and social and economic and philosophical movements of our day: as though humanity has learned nothing from the past; as though the human mind must always start all over again! Or perhaps you think that the ultimate tension between East and West which brought about the great schism of the eleventh century no longer holds; or that the Greeks and Latins love and trust each other now more than they did in 1054; or that the spirituality of the north is closer now to that of the south than it was in Luther's time; or that the north stomachs the Virgin Mary today more than it did before?

No, I am afraid the Christian today, if he is not blind, must bear in his own heart the lacerations of the Body of Christ, the scandals of division and estrangement; and he discovers in his own hesitations and calculations and fears and partial views rudiments of this same scandal.

He thus must fight day and night for the integrity and wholeness of his faith, not only against the whole gamut of modern heresies with which he rubs shoulders all the time, but against these same heretical and divisive tendencies and rudiments in his own soul.

III

There is therefore a thrust of God into history. All is calm and placid until the thrust intervenes. Creation is, as it were, subconscious and dormant until it is shaken and awakened by the hand of God. The thrust, the shaking, the awakening, takes place in two modes: the mode of promise under the old law when "the whole creation groaneth and travaileth in pain together" in earnest expectation of the manifestation of "the glorious liberty of the children of God"; and the mode of fulfillment under the new law when this "glorious liberty" is actually manifested through the Holy Spirit, and when therefore "there is no condemnation to them which are in Christ Jesus, who walk not after the flesh, but after the Spirit" (Romans 8). Whether as promise in the law or as fulfillment and manifestation in the Spirit and in faith, the thrust causes a tremendous disturbance, an unheard-of provocation, a scandalous offense. The Jew provokes and offends, and the Christian, if he is not hiding away his Christianity, also provokes and offends.

The world does not want to be reminded of its source: it is too much for it to see and hear God. Once created, creation balks at being recreated; it prefers rather to be uncreated. The Judaeo-Christian thrust alienates the world, because the world enjoys its alienness from God; because the world wants to be left alone, left wallowing in its own corruption, left in its own inherent drift towards nothingness. And so whether we speak of the Jew or of the Christian (and we had better speak of the Christian alone, because, as I believe, and as it is part of our faith, Paul having so wonderfully pointed it out in Romans, the Christian has already absorbed the Jew; he is either a metamorphosed Jew or a Gentile converted into the true Judaism according to God's promises; for the real Jew expects to be a Christian, he waits for becoming Christian, he is potentially a Christian perhaps as no one else is), I say, the Christian's appearance on the scene simply provokes, and he has to accept this result as his inevitable cross, knowing that just as the Spirit condemns, so it also justifies, just as there is Good Friday, so there is also Easter morn. The Christian must take the offense of the Cross in his stride: it should never frighten him or weaken his faith.

The deepest reason why there is and there can be no respite whatsoever in the fight of the Church — the fight against sin and imperfection in individual souls as well as the fight against heresies and deviations in whole movements — is the inevitable provocation of the thrust of God. Your very presence provokes; what is thus provoked kicks back and fights; therefore you have to fight back. You brought the fight upon your head, and you would have spared yourself every headache if either you were not present, or, being present, you managed to forget about Christ, by talking about science and education and peace and humanity and progress and universal brotherhood. And two things comfort and strengthen the Church in this self-induced wonderful fight: first, the simple fact that it was not the Church herself that brought about the thrust — it was God who freely decided and determined it Himself, and the world had to be provoked in consequence, and therefore you had no choice but to carry on the fight; and, secondly, the glorious fact that the Church is fighting, not in her own power, but with the Gospel filling her heart and mind and imagination, the Gospel which is in effect the sword of the Spirit, this very "Spirit [which] helpeth our infirmities . . . [and] maketh intercession for us with groanings which cannot be uttered," this very Spirit which assures us "that all things work together for good to them that love God" (Romans 8:26, 28).

"O the depth of the riches both of the wisdom and knowledge of God!" (Romans 11:33): how He creates, and at the same time does not forsake His creation, despite itself; how He "maketh sore, and bindeth up" (Job 5:18); how He "woundeth, and his hands make whole" (*ibid.*); how He stings and provokes, and at the same time draws all men unto Himself; how He makes us raise our fist in protest and rebellion, and at the same time causes us to break down in His arms in tears; how our sin becomes infinitely sharp and pointed in His presence, and at the same time He grants us His free forgiveness, a forgiveness we cannot bear and we do not understand; how He loads us with His Cross, and at the same time He carries it for us!

IV

The fight of the Church of Jesus Christ is eternal because that which brings about the provocation which causes the fight is itself the thrust of the eternal. We are always, then, at every step and in any circumstance whatsoever — whether in the strange personal drama of our soul, or from age to age throughout history, or as the Church appears in culture after culture and among people after people throughout the world, or as the Church fights error and darkness, or as opposition necessarily gathers and develops and the Church has to reckon with it — we are always dealing with the original thrust of God into a world offended and hurt. And if you think that the hurt feelings of the world, whether in you personally or in any culture brought up against the thrust and judgment of God, are going to be soothed and placated through diplomacy or classical music or education or culture or humanism or philanthropy or technical assistance or just being nice and reserved and inoffensive, or through the assurance that there is not going to be any nuclear war, then I am afraid you know neither yourself nor the world nor certainly the devil. Only the thrust itself which brought about the disturbance can calm it. Only the Cross which shocked and condemned the world can reconcile it. The Cross offends and scandalizes and the Cross alone can touch our touchy souls. God, it seems, took a great risk in dying on the Cross, the risk, namely, of heightening the offense to its nth degree; but despite this risk He had to die on the Cross in order to bring the world to its senses. It is impossible then to be ashamed of the Cross; for the Cross is offense and "foolishness" only "to them that perish"; but "unto us which are saved" and "unto them which are called," it is both "the power of God, and the wisdom of God" (I Corinthians 1).

The offense continues and so the preaching of the Cross must continue. There is no Church leader today who has real responsibility under Christ — I mean a Pope or a

Bishop or a simple Minister or Priest — and not only who
has responsibility but who feels it, and not only who feels
his responsibility but who does something about it, and
not only who has it and feels it and does something about
it, but whose conscience is deeply disturbed because he
knows, almost to the point of despair, how inadequate all
his doings are in the face of the massive onslaught of the
anti-Christian forces around him and within him: I say,
there is no responsible Church leader today who will not
time and again fall on his knees seeking light and guidance
and assurance at the feet of the Cross. There is no Church
leader who really knows what is happening and what
may still happen who can in good conscience pride himself
on anything save his faith in the crucified and risen Christ.

V

The constancy of God's assault is truly amazing. He
will not let the world go. You think He might relax with
the passage of time, but He doesn't. He impinges on you
today exactly as He did or will do when you were or will
be 12 or 20 or 40. The very twang of His impingement
tastes the same. He impinges upon the present world situation with all its possibilities, for good or for evil, exactly as
He did in the days of Moses or David or Paul or Constantine
or Charlemagne or Albert the Great or Napoleon; with this
decisive difference, however, that *after* Christ we are in the
presence of absolute fulfillment in history, and not only of
symbols and signs and sheer promise. But He who promised
is the same as He who fulfilled: it is one and the same
thrust. There is an incredible sameness about God throughout. The passage of time makes no difference, or rather it
makes only this difference: that time itself becomes de-

bunked. *Before* time has elapsed you still as it were give it the benefit of the doubt: you say, I don't know, it may make a difference. But after it has passed and, through the sameness of God's power, you realize that its passage has made no difference, it is debunked in your eyes. So the only difference the passage of time makes is to confirm that it makes no difference — and that is quite an important difference. In this way you are thrown back joyfully and thankfully upon the eternal God.

What is new is not anything in history or from history or from the world. What is new is always only two things: that there are always new men born in the world to whom the Gospel must be preached; and the specific response by these men to it. Man is eternal; so is God; and so is the Gospel. What is really new in history therefore is always the new man in Jesus Christ. The constancy of the thrust of God in our own lives and in its bearing upon the world is simply amazing. And, but for the resurrection of Jesus Christ, which is the only truly new and significant event in history, we could say that the constancy of human nature is equally amazing. There is a great mystery behind the equality of these two constancies.

As to the question of preaching the Gospel to the whole earth, I never cease to wonder at the disturbing statements which Paul keeps on repeating (for example in Colossians 1:6 and 1:23 and Romans 10:18 and 16:26) that that was already accomplished in his own day! I do not understand this to be only a manner of speaking. What was left unpreached to then is not much different from what is left unpreached to now. It is not necessary that literally every single human being should be preached the Gospel before

Paul's statements become true. There is a theologically significant sense in which it is true to say that the Gospel has been "preached to every creature which is under heaven"; even in Paul's time, certainly today. And it would seem there will always be people who have not had an adequate opportunity of being preached to, both in the sense of not having been reached physically and in the subtler sense of not having heard what is being preached to them. That is why the preaching of the Gospel, if only God opens our eyes and hearts, will always be news of the highest and most exciting order. In fact, the surest sign that God is speaking to us and we are listening is precisely when the Gospel strikes us as news of the highest and most exciting order. And as soon as it begins to sound dull and stale, we may take that as a sure sign that our heart has been shut to God.

VI

Who then can preach the Gospel? I think not any man. He alone can preach the Gospel who is called by God and through whom God can speak. But who is called by God and who is His mouthpiece? Only he to whom the Gospel radically speaks. Only he who allows it to analyze and judge his life. Only he who humbly and silently stands before its amazing story. Only he who confesses the guilt which it imputes to him. Only he who, gratefully accepting Christ's forgiveness, is cleansed of his sin and endowed from on high with the power of the Holy Ghost. Only he who acknowledges that exactly the same forces of darkness which slew our Lord long ago in Jerusalem are as operative in our own lives and times as they were in the lives and times of those who cried: "Crucify him, crucify him, his blood be on us and on our children!" — I mean the forces of bigotry, hatred, jealousy, fear, cleverness, the love of material things, preferring the world and its pleasures to Christ, the nationalism of the Jews, the imperialism of the Romans, the fury of the mob, the vested interests of the rulers and scribes and Pharisees, the timidity of the compromisers and cowards, the innate human inability to bear the sight of God.

He alone can preach the Gospel in such a way that through him then God speaks, who, allowing, confessing, and acknowledging all this, nevertheless accepts Christ's forgiveness of his sins. Life eternal begins with that act of acceptance. The mark of participation in the kingdom of God is precisely that act of acceptance. The power of God which he is then able to mediate, simply, directly, and without any effort on his part, is absolutely incredible. It is not he who acts, but the Holy Ghost. "Go ye and preach the Gospel" means simply "bring others to this same act of acceptance." Blessed are those who are called to this greatest of all honors. Blessed also are those who, doing other honorable things, wish they had been called to this greatest of all honors, and wish also that they were beginning their life anew to inquire from the Lord Jesus whether He would thus call them. And whether we are called to preach the Gospel of life and truth and being or we only wish we were called, let us live these days of our pilgrimage simply, quietly, humbly, trustingly, seeking, if possible, only the face of our Lord Jesus Christ, "to whom be glory and might, together with the Father and the Holy Ghost, now and always, even for ever and ever. Amen."

CHAPTER IV

THE GOSPEL AND THE LIFE OF THE SPIRIT

I

Conditions today appear to be most propitious for the life of the spirit. I doubt that they were so before, say, in the nineteenth century or early this century. Life then was too smooth, too placid, in a sense too innocent; there was no "need" therefore to penetrate beneath the surface. You could live a lifetime then without having to ask a fundamental question or face a fundamental issue. But today he must be a dead man or a thoroughly corrupt man who is not forced into the depths. And the more we go into the depths of the spirit, the more we understand the Gospel and the more we feel that every word in it, every turn of thought in it, every little incident in it, illuminates those depths and puts us in touch with the creative power of God. It would appear that no age was more cut to send the sincere seeker to the Gospel, where he will find his absolute fill, than this age, with all its untold problems and sufferings.

We are really at the end of a whole epoch of history, and we do not know what the new epoch is going to be. This is what makes the present moment most exciting. Everything today is at once an end and a beginning;

everything is critical and formative. In politics, in economics, in the international order, in the sense of security, in science, in fundamental thought, in religion, in man's own intimate relations to his creative energies — in these realms whole orders are dissolving and something new and as yet undetermined is dying to be born.

You trust perhaps in democracy and the liberty of man? But democracy and liberty today, even in the United States of America, are circumscribed by innumerable qualifications, rendering the individual human person less and less the master of his own political fate. The sense of individual impotence is most poignant when it comes to the real decisions that constitute history, with the result that nothing is more common today than the personal feeling of political frustration and helplessness. You gently but firmly drive home to people the immense sense of the crisis, and invariably they turn to you and say in utter sincerity: what can I as a human mortal *do*? And knowing the impotence of the individual person, out of sheer compassion on them you absolutely refuse to suggest fantastic formulae; usually all that comes to you to say is: go home, understand the truth, love God, and pray! And if this is the case in the land of liberty *par excellence,* what can one say about all other lands where, in varying degrees, the individual has little or nothing to do with his government? Therefore this political order that was supposed to be immutable is in a sense dissolving before our very eyes, and something new and as yet undetermined is rising on its ruins.

You trust perhaps in free enterprise? But need I point out to you that more than half of the world today knows nothing of this system, and that even in this country endless, and endlessly multiplying, are the pressures, the restrictions, the regulations, that qualify and limit the free economic process? If you desire not to close your eyes to the honest truth, you will at once perceive that "socialism" is invading every aspect of "capitalism," and you will acknowledge that all that can be done is to regulate, but not to reverse or arrest, this process. Therefore this economic order that was supposed to be immutable is in a sense dissolving before our very eyes, and something new and as yet undetermined is rising on its ruins.

You trust perhaps the present international order? But in a decade we have witnessed a tremendous revolution in this very order, with the consolidation and spread of Communism all over the world, with the rise of innumerable centers of independent self-will all over Asia, Africa and Latin America, and with the relative weakening and decline of the West; and the situation remains so fluid that nothing is more certain than that new orders, new balances, new configurations, new clashes, are everywhere now in process of emerging. Therefore here again something is dissolving, and something new and as yet undetermined is rising on its ruins.

You trust perhaps your armed forces to protect you and you rely on the oceans to keep the enemy away from you? But, lo, distance has been annihilated, and your enemies appear to have at their disposal weapons at least as mighty as your own. Therefore the order of physical and military safety is dissolving, and some new and as yet undetermined order of safety, or perhaps of unsafety, is rising on its ruins.

You trust perhaps in the findings and laws of science? But is any revolution today more revolutionary than what is happening to science and technology? Every day witnesses new marvels, new possibilities, for good or for evil, in physics and chemistry, in the exploration of space, and above all in the biological and social sciences, so that it is quite probable that, at this rate of development, present scientific ideas of matter, energy, life and the social process, and the technologies that are based on these ideas, shall appear, say, in a hundred years, as old-fashioned and primitive as the ideas of the ancient Egyptians and ancient Greeks appear to us today. Therefore a general dissolution seems to have overtaken the scientific order, with marvelous new knowledge and new technique arising, beyond any doubt, from the ashes of the old.

You trust perhaps one or another of the received philosophies? But whether it is idealism, or pragmatism, or criticism, or positivism, or humanism, or materialism, or scientism, or analysis, or existentialism — a pall of weariness and doubt is settling on them all. They appear to be in one world, and what is real and urgent and important and pressing and constitutive of life and history and truth, appears to be in another. There is a general philosophical bewilderment and confusion of the profoundest character; the mind is shaken at its foundations; and there is a desperate search for new principles even if these should turn out to be the forgotten principles of old. The phenomenon of philosophers having to demonstrate in the streets, in Paris and in London, and, who knows?, perhaps someday also even in Boston! — even if the demonstration is at times most unauthentic and childish — is most revealing as to philosophy's sudden realization how limited and unreal and abstract and insufficient it has been. Therefore in fundamental thought also something is dissolving, and something new and as yet undetermined is struggling to be born.

You trust perhaps the existing religious order? But the gods and religions of Asia are undergoing new and mighty reincarnations; Islam is actively planning a revival of spiritual energy and conquest, and conditions in Africa seem to be quite propitious for these plans; the Protestants are no longer very sure that endless proliferation is a good thing, and therefore how to stop and how to regroup is now the question; there is a distinct shift in theology away from rationalism and liberalism towards the faith of the Fathers, and less and less people are ashamed to confess the Creed and mean it; everybody — Protestant, Orthodox and Catholic — is talking and thinking of unity, and anxiously working for it; and new secular or atheistic religions are driving out the God of Abraham, of Isaac and of Jacob, who is the Father of our Lord Jesus Christ. Therefore the religious order, whether among the Christians or between the Christians and the non-Christians, is profoundly dissolving, and something new and as yet undetermined is rising on its ruins.

You trust perhaps the man of the Renaissance and the humanism of the Enlightenment? But it is fairly easy to show that the Renaissance has completely come to an end, and the Enlightenment, even if it had something to begin with, has completely exhausted itself. Rapturously enjoying the harmonies and beauties of nature, infinitely trusting himself and his powers, sinning without feeling a sense of guilt or shame, moulding the matter of his art — whether in painting or sculpture or poetry, or in the fashioning of states and the constructing of social orders — in ecstatic joy and perfect freedom, taking the sufferings and tragedies of life senselessly in his stride, and, as a result of all this, usurping in a sense the creative place of God — this type of man is no longer possible. Man today is not as simple, as innocent and as free as all that. He is much more self-entangled and self-conscious; he is much less sure of himself; he needs something outside himself (this has taken the form in most cases of society — "socialism" — or the state — "nationalism") to lean upon, to trust. And as to the Enlightenment, it is not difficult to show, from their thought and their action, and from the way they club and intrigue together, that those who claim to be still its children are enlightened only in the ways of bigotry, intolerance, cleverness, narrowness of vision, and hatred of all that is genuine and deep and true. Therefore here again we witness the two chief marks of the modern age dissolving before our very eyes, and something new and as yet inscrutable rising on their ruins.

It appears, then, that in the political order, in the economic order, in the international order, in the sense of security, in the scientific order, in the philosophical order, in the religious order, and in that most intimate identity of man with himself whereby he is confidently transported with the ecstatic joy of creation — in these realms — and, pray tell me, what is there left besides them? — in these realms the apocalyptic vision of "the first heaven and the first earth" "passing away" and of "a new heaven and a new earth" where there will be "no more sea" rising from their ashes — this vision appears to be literally true today; only we cannot be as sure as St. John was that, while "the former things are passed away," the new order of things shall be "the holy city, new Jerusalem, coming down from

God out of heaven," the city where God shall dwell with men and "shall wipe away all tears from their eyes" (Revelation 21).

II

Three fundamental questions arise: (a) What is this new thing that is being born? (b) Where is Christ in it? And (c) what is our role, both severally and collectively, in its self-formation?

It is at this point — in honestly and absolutely facing these three shattering questions — that the depths of the life of the spirit begin to reveal themselves. Having fully realized that the whole world is as it were dissolving before our very eyes, it is impossible then to ask more far-reaching questions than: what is then emerging, where is Christ in it, and what difference are we making to the whole thing? In the dreadful anguish which attends these questions — *if only we understood them* — we are forced to descend to the deepest depths of our being; we immediately fall on our knees and put on sackcloth and ashes. And if at these deepest depths we find only the silly, the sentimental, the stupid, the subjective; if we find only jokes and anecdotes and dreams and selfish interests; if we find nothing that rings true to the eternal, nothing that Paul and Peter and the Virgin Mary and the great saints would fully understand and applaud, saying "Well-done!, now we know you are worthy of your calling;" if we find nothing that touches God Himself authentically, nothing that we absolutely know flows from Him — if this is what we find and this is what we do not find at our deepest depths — then we know nothing of the life of the spirit, and then we can neither raise these anxious questions nor certainly can we answer them. To see that the world as we have known it is dissolving and that "all things are being made new," to see where Christ is in this process, and to have something to do with it ourselves, all this is not something mechanical, external, abstract, intellectual, marginal to our existence: all this requires the deepest spiritual life possible to stupid and mortal man. And since we can never attain these depths of the spirit by ourselves — for this is not a matter of psychology or introspection or analysis or moral resolution or hard work or rich experience — it takes the positive, active, actual intervention of God in our life — *from outside, from His own mysterious freedom* — to bring us to the deepest depths of which we are capable and therefore to open before us the ultimate questions of this age and the role we can and should play in them. To say that this age, of all ages, is most propitious for the life of the spirit is then precisely to say that, because "the first heaven and the first earth" are passing away, and "a new heaven and a new earth" are taking their place, we can never understand what is happening, much less can we do anything about it in Christ and for Christ, unless we enter fully into the deepest mysteries of the life of the spirit, with all the unspeakable sufferings and all the unutterable glories that such a life necessarily entails. In this age, of all ages, the full life of the spirit is a greater necessity than food or drink or air or the smile of your child. And I tell you what amazes me more than anything else: it is how people can, with the obvious dissolution and recreation of the world, any longer stand living anywhere save in the depths where they are literally with God and in God.

III

Some people — even some Christians — who have been impressed by the present universal dissolution have tended to conclude that everything, including Jesus Christ, is caught up in the soulless flux. Christian morals, Christian doctrine, the Sacraments, the Church, Jesus Christ Himself — all these things will be "outgrown." The present historical conflagration is going to burn up even Christ and His Church. But these people either have never known Christ at all, or, having once known Him and then, for some reason, rebelled against Him, they wish that He too would be consumed by the universal fire. I may remark in passing that they never quite tell us what will replace Him after He and His Church are consumed and "outgrown;" they yield the distinct impression that they do not give a hoot for what replaces Him provided only He is gotten out of the way! A deeper insight into the mysteries of the present moment in history could reveal (and I believe it would reveal) that behind much of the impulse for so-called revolution and change is a profound anti-Christian desire to get rid of Christ altogether. The hatred of the very name of Christ, which could take exceedingly sophisticated and subtle forms wholly unrecognizable by the innocent and gullible, is at the base of a good deal of what is happening in the world today. He does not live in this age who does not smell this hatred all around him, even among his friends. But those who know Christ and remain faithful to Him know that He alone stands above the flux and beyond it; they know that He is "the same yesterday, and today, and for ever" (Hebrews 13:8); they see Him very clearly — I mean with the wonderful clarity of faith — as the Lord of history, and therefore not only as the judge, but even as "the cause" of the universal dissolution; they see Him therefore, not only above and beyond the flux, but even "behind" it; they understand perfectly — I mean with the wonderful understanding of faith — what the Evangelist means when he affirms that "all things were made by him; and without him was not any thing made that was made" (John 1:3) and what the Apostle means when he exultantly proclaims that not only by Him God "made the worlds" but that "all things" are now being upheld by "the word of his power" (Hebrews 1:2-3); they "know whom [they] have believed, and [are] persuaded that he is able to keep that which [they] have committed unto him against that day" (II Timothy 1:12). I repeat: not any man can say these things, but only he who lives in the depths, only he who fully knows Jesus Christ, only he who has died (and in this life we die, deaths many and diverse!, including perhaps actual physical death, for who can be sure that he never actually physically died and Christ thereupon revived him without his knowing it?; in my simplicity I believe this *can* happen and *has in fact* happened many times!) and has been mightily raised by Him. Let the devil therefore rage and rave and rant as much as he pleases: one thing is not going to be dissolved, and that is Jesus Christ and His Holy and Apostolic Church. In his Divine Liturgy Saint John Chrysostom makes the Priest "ascribe" scores of times to Jesus Christ — always of course with the Father and the Holy Ghost — "glory, honour and worship," not only "now" and not only "for ever," but "from all Ages to all Ages."

IV

What now is this life of the spirit which in this age of great crisis is no longer a luxury — even if it were a luxury in any bygone age — and without which we cannot understand the character of the crisis, neither can we really be profitable in it?

Surely I am not going to give you a strange, elaborate, obscure, involved, dark, metaphysical answer to this question, an answer perhaps on the model of Hegel. Such men know only the life of the mind, the wonderful play and interplay of ideas in their reason. This is a very great and real life indeed. But we are asking here something much more radical: we are asking about the life of existence, namely, the life which faces at every moment either being or death. One of the meanings of the present world crisis — perhaps its deepest meaning — is that everywhere and in every way it is forcing us to face *existence at all,* namely, to seek that which has *created us out of nothing.* Creation, the creator, nothingness — these are the real themes today. This is the theological significance of contemporary existentialism; whether or not they know it, the existentialists are in effect *seeking their creator.*

In one word: the life of the spirit is *life in Jesus Christ.* In Him and through Him we can raise and answer the three fundamental questions. In Him and through Him we can be saved from the universal dissolution of the world.

Now Jesus Christ suffered and died on the Cross and rose from the dead on the third day. Therefore the life of the spirit, which is life in Jesus Christ, is a life of intense suffering and struggle. I laugh when people who are not Christian say that they are struggling. Let me therefore state it dogmatically: only he who has been touched by Jesus Christ knows what it means really to struggle and to suffer; and whoever is really struggling and suffering, even though he says he does not believe in Christ and has never heard of Him, has been nevertheless touched by Him, no matter how distantly or indirectly or strangely. But the flabby and fat, the soft and adjusted, the decadent and satisfied, those who always choose the line of least resistance, those who avoid every suffering, every struggle, every hardship, every effort, always, to be sure, with the most perfect rationalization, those who have never been crucified, and crucified indeed for the sake of Christ, those who have not seen the devil with his three hoofs and seven horns — these know nothing of the depths of the spirit and of the power of Christ to snatch us out of hell itself. It is these who are going to be consumed by the fire of history, leaving not even the trace of mere existence behind them.

Because always it is life or death that we face in the depths, the life of the spirit is a life of unending struggle. You know you must continue to be — and to be at your highest. In Jesus Christ we never cease struggling. I beg you therefore never to envy the saints, thinking that they were above the struggle of the spirit; envy them rather because, doomed to perpetual struggle, they never gave up. This is their miracle, this is their crown of glory, that every morning, despite the anguish of the day and night before, they rise up to resume the struggle, undaunted and undismayed. It is for this that I envy them: that they *never* give up — I wish I could convey to you what this word "never" means — they *never* let the world and their defeats at its hands get the better of them, they

always start all over again, even though it be always again
from zero, trusting Him who can always recreate them
from nothing. Since it is completely beyond their human
power *never* to give up, it follows — if only you knew the
quality and intensity of their struggle! — that they *never*
give up only because God Himself, somehow and for some
reason, *never* lets them go.

V

We struggle on at least six fronts. We struggle, first,
on the front of the world and its temptations, this world
which is so exciting, so colorful, so seductive, so sweet,
so delicious, so delectable, so real, so wonderful, that we
are always in danger of losing ourselves in it and forgetting
about Jesus Christ. We struggle, second, against our own
memories, those strange whisperings in the dark which
ever want to keep us captive to themselves. We struggle,
third, against that sweet, natural tendency in us to be
lazy and slothful, to covet more than we need, to expect
from life more than we give it; against that awful dissipation whereby we cease to be integral, whole, entire, uni-
fied, one. We struggle, fourth, against our inveterate pride,
that creaturely raising of ourselves above ourselves, that
blasphemous pitting of ourselves against God, that pitiful
refusal to let go — in humor, in brokenness and in tears.
We struggle, fifth, against our daily fall in the worship of
things and objects — the worship of ourselves, our name,
our beauty, our strength, our ideas, our cleverness, our
possessions, our country, our culture; in short, against the
worship of perishing and corrupt creatures, whose meaning
can never be understood apart from the living God who
created them. Finally, we struggle daily against the devil

himself; the devil who always lures us by the three temptations of security, magic and power; the devil who almost succeeds — in fact, apart from the repeated interventions of Christ, he always succeeds — in *proving* to us that there is no God, no Christ and no Holy Spirit.

The active life of the spirit is a life of constant struggle. Knowing the human condition in which we are thrown — and we know it only through Christ and in Christ — we seek with God's power to overcome this condition. If we yield to the seductiveness of the world, the struggle means that we soon rise and put the world in its place. If we lend an ear to past memories, the struggle means that we soon brush them aside and remember only the wonderful gift of God in Jesus Christ. If we wallow in slothfulness and dissipation, the struggle means that our lost integrity soon calls us back and we respond with tears at the feet of the Cross. If we are puffed up with pride, the struggle means that the next turn in the road will soon show us how silly, how unimportant, how fragile, how ugly, how hollow, how stupid, how indefensible, we are, and thus shattered to pieces, we soon pick ourselves up in brokenness and contrition, and often with a strange, sweet smile, thanking Jesus Christ, not for ourselves and our virtues, but for Himself alone. If we worship creatures and things, the struggle means that some faint echo of God the Creator will soon bring us back to our senses, usually when these creatures and things are melting away before our very eyes. And when the devil insinuates and whispers, the struggle means that, no matter how much we listen and fall to his disgusting wiles, we quickly take up the "shield of faith, wherewith we shall be able to quench all the fiery darts of the wicked" (Ephesians 6:16).

VI

He who has known the fullness of the power of God in Jesus Christ, he who has tasted something of this fullness of power in his own life, will always suffer and struggle. He can never forget what he has known and tasted: it holds him transfixed in its hands. "My heart is fixed, O God," cries David, "my heart is fixed: I will sing and give praise" (Psalm 57:7 and 108:1). If any moment arrives when he is not struggling, then something disastrous has happened to him. He is then settled, he is adjusted, forgetting that there can be no adjustment while God is there and the world and its passions are there. Really to know God is absolutely and necessarily to struggle and to suffer, because as fallen creatures, there is always "no health in us." We desperately crave for Him from the bottom of our heart, but we always fall far short of Him. But, thank God!, we can never forget Him, because He always reminds us of Himself. Why is the life of the spirit a life of perpetual struggle and suffering? Because God and the world are both beckoning it; because Christ and the devil are both appealing to it; because God and His glory is absolutely real, and our human nature and all it has come to mean is absolutely real; because it can never forget what it has known and tasted, and yet everything about it conspires to make it forget; because without God it cannot rise to Him, whereas all it has to do to settle comfortably in this world is to open its eyes and let itself go; because it lives in this world by sight and experience, whereas it lives in the other world, the wonderful world of Christ and the saints, by faith and by hope; because the enemies of Christ, in the soul of man and at large in the world, are never going to stop their darts and their attacks until He comes again.

It is in this endless struggle that the life of the spirit is lived and perfected. "For all the day long have I been plagued, and chastened every morning" (Psalm 73:14), and it is "through sufferings" that we are made "perfect" (Hebrews 2:10). The depths the life of the spirit reaches are infinite and beyond description. Only God knows them. It is enough to say that in them it sees God Himself, and at least as often the devil himself. Sometimes what it sees and feels in the twinkling of an eye it takes it a year to expound — and I mean "the twinkling of an eye" and I mean "a year" — and it can never do justice to it. Sometimes its tongue is tied, its mind is numbed, its hands are paralyzed, from the intensity of the brilliance it sees; and then it would not open its mouth while the world lasts. All you have to do to understand what I mean is to think of the Psalms of David, the Epistles of Paul, the writings of Augustine, the homilies of Chrysostom, the sufferings of Teresa, and the torments of Dostoyevsky. These men and women saw what no human eye has seen. The besetting temptation of the life of the spirit is simply to quit — the struggle being so unbearable and the suffering so intense. But it cannot quit, because none other than God is holding it. And if this is its temptation, its prize, if only it perseveres, is the vision of God and the certainty of God. "To him that overcometh will I give to eat of the hidden manna, and will give him a white stone, and in the stone a new name written, which no man knoweth saving he that receiveth it" (Revelation 2:17).

To one who lives in the depths everything else appears

silly and superficial. He cannot treat it with contempt, not because it is beneath contempt, but because the life of suffering rises above contempt: it has seen so much that it will look down upon nothing. But he can only treat it either with absolute silence, or with the most stinging irony. Irony is the only mode of communication from the depths.

The Gospel is the only road to the depths. Everything else is silly by comparison. With all his infinite cares and responsibilities, Saint John Chrysostom used to read the Epistles of Paul alone "twice every week, and often three or four times." If we lose ourselves one-hundredth as much in the Gospel, we will reach depths of knowledge and experience that we can reach in no other way. But the Gospel is not just a book; the book is about Jesus Christ who sits now on the right hand of the Father and who operates now through the Holy Ghost in the Church. That which the book is about is more important than the book: in fact it is its Author! The Gospel then is the road to The Way. The Gospel leads us to Christ Himself, and to what He has done and meant in history. It is in communion with the saints who read the Gospel and expounded it and fought the good fight and lived the life of the spirit and descended to the depths and served the Church that we can truly live the life of the spirit at its deepest depths. An hour of communion with David or Paul or Augustine or Chrysostom, on the level on which they thought and existed, and in their understanding of Christ, and in our and their understanding of what He meant to them in their own lives, is worth a century of stupid human gossip.

VII

Grounded in the Gospel and its infinite amplitude, struggling daily at the depths, communing daily with the saints in what Christ concretely meant to them, and living daily the active and responsible life of the Church with all its commitments and all its Sacraments — such a person alone can comprehend what is really happening today. By seeing Christ, in this day of judgment, sitting in judgment upon the universal dissolution of this age, he can have some notion of what is likely to emerge from the ruins of the old, and he can form some idea of his own humble, little role in it.

Chastened by his sufferings and therefore filled with the mind of Christ, he can readily see why the political, economic and international orders are dissolving — because there is so much injustice, so much falsehood, so much deception, so much guile, so much cunning, so much cleverness, so much callousness, so much inequality, so much arbitrariness, so much inhumanity, so much hypocrisy, so much pharisaism about them: in short, because they do not conform to the mind of Christ, and what does not conform to the mind of Christ must dissolve and disappear.

Even the order of security is unjust, because why should one country and one people alone be secure and the rest left as it were to the dogs?; because such things as "luck," "chance," "fortune" and "fate" are absolutely against the will and mind of Christ — at least if enjoyed selfishly and gloatingly, and without the deepest sense of responsibility to the Lord who would disown us unless when "the least of these (his) brethren" (and this means, not only in our neighborhood, not only in our nation, but everywhere, and therefore beyond all "fortune" and "luck") is hungry, we give him meat; or thirsty, we give him drink; or a stranger, we take him in; or naked, we clothe him; or sick, we visit him; or in prison, we minister unto him without calculation and fear (Matthew 25:31ff.).

Chastened by his sufferings and therefore filled with the mind of Christ, the Christian who is grounded in the Gospel and who lives the life of the spirit at its deepest depths can show that in the general scientific revolution there is a profound Christian significance, both in the details of its material contents and in the sharpening of the sense of moral responsibility from the decisions which this revolution forces upon man.

In philosophy it is the departure from the standpoint of God and being, it is the reliance upon arbitrary perspectives and willful human beginnings, that have brought about the universal intellectual collapse.

Chastened by his sufferings and therefore filled with the mind of Christ, the Christian living at the depths asks: why should there not be a dissolution of the religious order, seeing that the Gospel, thanks partly to the wonderful American missionary saga of the last century and a half, has been preached all over the world, challenging the non-Christian religions to bring forth whatever truth and value they harbor in their bosom, and seeing that the Christians are, partly by the direct pressure of Christ himself, partly by the increasing pressure of world conditions, at last fed up with their squabbles and their rivalries?

And in the crisis of humanism and art he sees the hand

of Christ reminding man of his finitude and of his essential dependence, even in the exercise of his natural creative energies, upon God his Creator.

VIII

The times are propitious for the deepest life of the spirit. The general dissolution all over the world is crying to be understood and interpreted. What is more, it is crying to be utilized and directed in the service of Christ. "The harvest truly is plenteous" as never before: "pray ye therefore the Lord of the harvest" to send forth laborers into his field (Matthew 9:37, 38).

More depends upon American Christianity today than perhaps upon any other Christianity in history, though certainly not more than upon the Christianity of the Apostles. This is a tremendous honor that the Christians of America can only accept with humility and gratitude. You have no idea how much every one in this room, no matter how humble, can make a decisive difference to the course of events — if only he prays enough, and suffers enough, and believes enough, and loves enough, and goes deeply enough into the life of the spirit, and appropriates enough the Gospel and Jesus Christ, "the author and finisher of our faith" (Hebrews 12:2), into his soul. May it therefore be God's will that, while everything today is in a state of flux, your prayers, your efforts, sincere and genuine and humble as they are, will help in redeeming what is redeemable in this dissolving world, to the end that God the Father shall be glorified, and the name of Jesus Christ through the Holy Ghost shall be lifted above every other name.

CHAPTER V

FAITH IN JESUS CHRIST

I

In the spiritual life one must catch himself where he is and speak from there. It is silly to start from anywhere else. Other stands land you only in abstraction, remoteness, and insincerity. But the life of the spirit is freedom and lightness of heart. Therefore let your present spiritual state speak, and with its speaking I beg you to laugh. Don't strain at something distant and abstruse and far away. You are not real as you do so. You have plenty right before you to speak from and about.

Nothing is closer to our life than faith in Jesus Christ. If we have it, we know how crucially important it is in our lives; if we do not have it, we live enstranged in a state of permanent torment. If we have it or if we do not have it, faith in Jesus Christ is the first and last meaning of our life. I do not care who or what you are; I put only one question to you: Do you believe in Jesus Christ? If you believe in Him, then even though you are slandered and abused and misunderstood and miserable, even though you are dying, even though you are in hell, you will shed a few tears on your knees and, arising, you will gradually mount to heaven where the angels sing.

And if you do not believe in Him, then even though you are in heaven, even though you are the happiest and most secure person, I am afraid for you.

In the anguished cry of the father of the child with a dumb spirit, "Lord, I believe; help thou mine unbelief" (Mark 9:24), we have the perfect expression of the dialectic of faith. For faith in Jesus Christ is not something we acquire once and for all and then carry for the rest of our lives in the manner in which we carry our bodies or the color of our eyes; faith in Jesus Christ is being constantly put to the test; it is daily under trial; we have perpetually to reacquire it again and again. Thus we cannot take pride in our faith as though it were thanks to us that we had it or continue to have it; we must always turn to Him and say with the Apostles: "Lord, increase our faith" (Luke 17:5). For without His faithfulness we will forthwith become faithless.

II

One trial of our faith is when we consider that after two thousand years the world is still so much unchristian and the Christians themselves are so faithless and so unworthy of the glorious name they bear. In their protected sentimental complacency people do not know what I am talking about. They must come out of their comfortable shells into the wide open world to get the shock of their lives. The world with which we have to deal is largely unchristian and even anti-Christian. Our faith in Jesus Christ is very childish indeed (would that it were childlike!) until we find ourselves in the position of David who tells us that after God had "looked down from heaven upon the children of men, to see if there were any that did understand, that did seek God," He found that "every one of them is gone back: they are altogether become filthy; there is none that doeth good, no, not one" (Psalm 53:2, 3). Our faith in Jesus Christ is very rudimentary indeed (would that it were primary!) until we find ourselves crying with David, "Help, Lord; for the godly man ceaseth; for the faithful fail from among the children of men" (Psalm 12:1); with Isaiah, "Lord, how long?" (Isaiah 6:11); and with John, "Even so, come, Lord Jesus" (Revelation 22:20). We should first absorb the shock that the Lord is somehow tarrying, that the world will always be largely unchristian, that the faithful will always be a very small minority, and that none of us can be absolutely sure that he belongs to that minority, before our faith is truly confirmed in us. Our faith must predicate itself upon and accept these four facts before it becomes real faith, before it begins to merit any reward.

When we really take in the radical character of this situation we can then only trust the mercy of God. Faith is to live on this radical trust of His mercy. The problem of the election and the remnant and the Church becomes then a burning issue in our life. For all their obscurity, pitfalls and dangers, these matters must be fearlessly faced. Paul and Augustine and Calvin and Karl Barth were not talking nonsense when they had to wrestle with them, however we may agree or disagree with some of their conclusions; yet of the four, with Paul at least I cannot say that I am in a position or ever shall be in a position to "disagree." Man is free, yes; but God is even more free; and it seems to be His pleasure to hold some men captives for Him more than others. There is an unfathomable mystery here, very much like the "unspeakable words, which it is not lawful for a man to utter" (II Corinthians 12:4) which that strange friend of Paul's had heard in the third heaven.

To live in a modicum of peace in this world, a Christian, for all his zeal, for all his missionary drive, for all his burning desire in obedience to the Lord to convert all men and all nations, for all his kindliness and gentleness and piety, must nevertheless accept the sad lot of belonging to a permanent minority. Did you hear?! — I said *permanent* minority! This should not disturb him because the possession of Christ and the fellowship of the Holy Spirit compensate for the loss of the whole world. His deepest joy and sorrow at the same time is that the others do not have the vaguest idea what they are living without. Faith must undergo and survive this bitter test. And when we affirm with Paul from the bottom of our heart, "That at the name of Jesus every knee should bow, of things in heaven, and things in earth, and things under the earth; and that every tongue should confess that Jesus Christ is Lord, to the glory of God the Father" (Philippians 2:10, 11), we do so in humble but certain faith.

III

Unless we pass this fiery test and hold fast to our faith, we might fall into another temptation which could fritter away all our faith or whatever of it was left in us. We might become too much preoccupied with the world and its problems. Christians at times get themselves overworked about the state of the world. This is not a sign of faith but of the exact opposite. They should relax and trust Christ more. And so we set about, with the best of intentions, no doubt, and calling upon the power of

Christ, to save the world from prejudice, ignorance, backwardness, corruption, injustice, war, sin: in short, from the grip of the devil. Christians in position of responsibility, whether civil or ecclesiastical, must certainly try to do all this; they cannot face their Lord in His day having been unprofitable and delinquent in their tasks. But it is one thing to go about saving the world, or the humblest of situations in it, in our own human power, and it is an entirely different thing to trust that act of salvation to God, while meantime doing everything we can in obedience to His will. It is one thing to be nervous and worried and concerned and unsure, and it is an entirely different thing to let Christ Himself accomplish His work in us and through us — calmly, quietly, surely, and almost without giving His using us a thought ourselves. But it is eminently possible to lose oneself in the cares and worries of the world and therewith to lose Christ. The cry of "Martha, Martha" (Luke 10:41) keeps ringing in my ears when I behold people, including above all myself, busy day and night trying to save the world; especially as I am not sure that in our business we are adoring Christ enough; and our adoration of Him is the most important thing possible.

Moreover, there are cases where, no matter how much we may fret and fume, we can really do nothing ourselves, or what we can do is exceedingly limited in efficacy. Things as it were must take their own natural course, which might include the possibility of the manifestation of the judgment of God. We can then only ardently pray for His compassion. History is full of instances where God had to manifest His wrath despite every human effort and good will. This is Paul's verdict on paganism in Romans.

We can only trust God's justice and pray for His mercy. And where that is obviously the case, we are only frittering away our energies and wasting our substance by worrying too much or smiting our breast too severely. There is a divine economy whereby we may conserve our resources for the most telling impact, upon the most promising soil, at the most opportune moment.

It is perfectly clear that we can save nobody and nothing if we are not first sure of ourselves. In these matters we can never bluff, we can never hide away our truth. To have the world maddeningly on our mind all the time is not the way to be sure of ourselves. It is rather the way to be distracted, to be unsure, to be impotently spread all over, for the world is completely uncontrollable and there is absolutely no end to what can and should be saved. The dike of corruption cannot be plugged at every point, because the points are infinite. It is enough if an oasis of health here and another there can be secured. And so to be busy at this point and that point and that other point is often the way of escaping and fleeing from ourselves and therefore from Christ. It appears that the contemplative method of Mary is preferable. When I meet a soul hailing from a life of profound contemplation and prayer I immediately feel that the whole world is being there and then saved at his or her feet. I think it is the Marys more than the Marthas who are going to save the world, although the Marthas are indispensable in the process.

Only those who stay very close to Christ can help others who are far away. Only those who prefer Him to everything else, even to the call of the needy world, can be used by Him for the need of the world. Only those who are not lifted by pride to suppose that they must carry the whole burden of the world will be pitied by Him, who does in fact carry the whole burden of the world, and given a humble part of that burden to carry with Him. Only those who go through one hell after another without losing sight of Him — because even "if I make my bed in hell, behold, thou art there" (Psalm 139:8) — will be granted the power, not in their time, but in His time, to help the world out of the several hells in which it finds itself.

The victory of Christ in our lives is the greatest thing and in the end the only thing for which we should be thankful. Our faith is never more keenly tested than when, thinking we are going to save the world, we really set about — whether seriously or half in jest — to save it. A sense of humor is of the essence of faith, and the deeper the mystery of faith, the more refined and lively the sense of humor. And we are quite without humor about ourselves when, forsaking the way of Mary, we readily follow in the footsteps of Martha.

IV

And yet Christians live in the world and Christ never meant them to live out of it. "I pray not that thou shouldest take them out of the world, but that thou shouldest keep them from the evil" (John 17:15). In the world they must work out their own salvation and as much of the salvation of the world as possible. They cannot wash their hands of what is going on in the world. On the contrary, they must take the most active interest in it. Of none has this been more true than of American Christianity, with its wonderful missionary epic, ventured forth and accomplished purely in the name of Jesus Christ. What a crown of glory has this Christianity laid up for itself as a result of its prayers and exertions and vision and loving sacrifice and service all over the world!

Now the importance of the emergence of Asia and Africa from the Christian point of view is threefold. First, it is good and proper that these nations take their destinies in their own hands. A Christian can only rejoice at the sight of people realizing and exercising their dignity and independence. Second, new perfections of the spirit are called for to work out the proper creative fellowship between equals. The fellowship of equals is the end of all fellowship, and therefore it should be looked upon as the norm and rule. Once perfected it becomes far more stable and enriching. And third, Christians under the new conditions will have to demonstrate their faith in Jesus Christ in the teeth of five trials. (a) They have to stand firm as they face the resuscitated tribal and national deities. (b) They have to stand firm as they see old great religions rediscovering and reasserting themselves. (c) They have to work out new creative dialogues based on our common human nature and need. (d) Their own governments often find themselves embarrassed by them and by Christ. Now, the Church should never meddle in political affairs; she should never make the truth of the Gospel dependent upon the fortunes, which are more often misfortunes, of systems and regimes and persons. But in the impersonal formal order of international relations, Christians could find themselves a cause of embarrassment to their own governments. This is their trial and their cross, and they should bear it courageously, keeping in mind that governments and politics and cultures come and go, but Jesus Christ endureth forever.

And (e) alien anti-Christian movements also have to
be faced. It could be said a hundred years from now, it
might be said in heaven right now, that the Christians,
whether by default or by folly or by sheer stupidity or
because they were comfortable and relaxed, lost in the
competition for the soul of Asia and Africa in the sixties
of the twentieth century. For this is a most crucial decade.
We can only say with Paul, God forbid! But let me tell
you, there are situations in which the issue is very delicately
poised. The Christian debacle in China is a sobering
warning. I am not thinking of competition between political
systems: that is an affair of governments, and that is a
realm completely other than what I am here thinking of,
a realm with its own honorable rules, rhythms and laws. I
am thinking of the competition for the soul and mind of the
people. I am thinking of whether Christians, not governments, can relax if the mind of the people is poisoned with
respect to the name of Jesus Christ. Mighty forces are
moving fast into whole spiritual vacua. Surely history will
say a hundred years from now — in so far as there will
be true history then — surely heaven is saying right now,
what was the matter with the Christians, where were they?
Nothing therefore is more necessary than to arouse responsible Christians from their lethargy and slumber into
both the infinite dangers and the infinite possibilities of
the moment.

At the heart of the whole matter is faith in Jesus Christ.
Do we believe in Him as passionately as others believe in
their own ideas and systems? If we do, then we ought
to do better than they. For we worship a Person, they
worship an idea. We worship Life and Strength and Love
and Victory; they worship negation and hatred. Christ can

do without us; He can raise up children to Abraham from these stones; He may be secretly doing so already in the vast spaces of Asia and Africa. And so if we fail Him, it cannot be that He failed; we will only have proven that we are unprofitable servants. Nothing puts our faith to the ultimate test more than the concrete challenge facing us all in Asia and Africa today.

V

The Christians all over the world are now more mingling and dealing with other religions and outlooks and points of view than ever before. Here lurks another trial. Their faith could be easily overwhelmed and overawed by the gods and religions and mythologies of Asia and Africa, as well as by the new fads and outlooks sprouting in the West. Jesus Christ becomes one among many. He becomes even a weak one, one of whom we might be ashamed. We begin to see the good in these other outlooks — and there is plenty of it — and we lose our hold on Christ, or, better, He lets go His hold on us. The result is confusion, uncertainty, and loss or attenuation of faith. They tell an apocryphal story of a Pope in the Middle Ages sending two friars to convert the Chinese. Some catastrophe happened which cut off the two priests entirely from the home base, and everybody in Rome thought they were dead. Twenty years afterwards two Buddhist monks appeared in Rome and requested an audience with the Pope. The Chamberlain noticed that they knew Latin perfectly and, becoming curious, he managed to arrange an interview for them. When they met the Pope he asked them how it was that they knew Latin so well. They explained to him that they were the two Catholic friars whom his predecessor of blessed memory had sent to China twenty years before. He was happy to receive them but before the interview was over the Pope discovered that the whole point of their visit was to try to convert him to Buddhism. The story does not tell whether they succeeded. You and I must know of cases where people began with the stoutest Christian faith, with the purest and noblest Christian intentions, but upon prolonged mixing and exposure and living with other religions and cultures, they ended with the haziest notion of Jesus Christ and began to preach some vague eclectic or pantheistic or humanitarian form of religion.

It is a bounden Christian duty to love and serve our fellow men, whether Christian or unchristian; indeed to love and serve our enemies. It is our sacred duty to promote justice, give everybody his due, educate the ignorant, tend the sick, recognize the good everywhere, and salvage and rejoice in the truth wherever we find it and regardless of the error and darkness in which it may be embedded and with which it may be overlaid. The Lord said to Jeremiah, "If thou take forth the precious from the vile, thou shalt be as my mouth" (Jeremiah 15:19). Surely we are to identify the precious everywhere and take it forth from the vile to become like unto the mouth of God. But if the price we pay for all this is loss of faith in Jesus Christ, estrangement from His presence, then that is too heavy a price, at least because without Him we cannot love our enemies, or serve kinsman and stranger alike, or really know what justice is, or really recognize truth and goodness wherever we find them. When I see all this attempted without faith, I wonder if it is not all sentimental and human and political; and these will not only soon decay and degenerate, but they can never be sure of them-

selves. If Jesus Christ exists, and if He is what we believe
Him to be, what He Himself says He is, and what our
fathers have for two thousand years handed Him down
to us as being, then I can only be loving and helpful and
just and profitable to others through Him and in Him and
with Him. I certainly do not expect this to be understood
by diplomats or politicians or businessmen or philanthro-
pists or educators who are not also Christians; I expect it
to be understood by Christians who know and believe in
Jesus Christ, whatever else they might also be.

Time and experience constitute a sort of demon. With
time the sharpness of the original conviction is lost. One
becomes sophisticated and cynical. He is no longer of
one mind: he is now of many. "Many things" he must
take into consideration, "many things" he must keep in
mind. One therefore often wonders whether it were not
far better for some who thus become "wise" if they had
died young. Which is better, a life ending early (say, at
the age of 33 or 44) in a youth of conviction and firmness,
or a life ending late (say, at the age of 66 or 88) in an old
age of flabbiness and cynicism? One wonders. How to
exorcise this terrible demon, how to overcome the "matur-
ing wisdom" of age and time, how to retain in all its
sharpness the original flame of innocency and faith and
conviction — all this is a very great problem. It raises
issues of a dozen different fundamental orders: personal
fate, the place of personal effort, the problem of election,
the problems of physiology and of the laws of nature,
the laws of the spirit, the independent life of the spirit,
the authority of the Church, the place of the Liturgy and
the Sacraments, the historic-existential source of the flame,
how one may authentically replenish his soul, how one

may be periodically born anew, in short, the whole problem of the devil. There was a time in our life perhaps when we absolutely and unreservedly and intuitively believed with Peter that "there is none other name under heaven given among men, whereby we must be saved" (Acts 4:12), and with Paul that "other foundation can no man lay than that is laid, which is Jesus Christ" (I Corinthians 3:11), but then "the cares of this world" (Matthew 13:22, Mark 4:19, Luke 8:14) gradually made us "wise" and "choked" this conviction in our soul. The problem of faith is how to exorcise this awful demon of time and nature and experience and "wisdom" and doubt, especially when the "wisdom" and the doubt arise from contact with other religions, other fundamental outlooks and other absolute claims. The Holy Ghost does it wonderfully.

VI

There is another trial, or better another challenge, of our faith which has been tormenting me lately. Saint John says that the eternal Word of God, which was also God, "was made flesh . . . dwelt among us" and was "full of grace and truth" (John 1:14); that this very Word of God which "was made flesh" is Jesus Christ; and that "all things were made by him" (John 1:3). We repeat this in the Creed every Sunday when we say that through Jesus Christ "all things were made." Now I confess when I say these things I believe them from the bottom of my heart with the utmost firmness. But these are tremendous assertions. Do we really believe them? What do they mean? How can it be that Jesus Christ created you and me and Plato and Julius Caesar and the stars and the oceans and the science of economics and this table and the mole on yonder person's face, or that the creator of these things took two thousand years ago the form of Jesus of Nazareth? There is a challenge, then, to show how this is the case, to make this terrific affirmation a bit reasonable. I think if we take our faith seriously, we owe it to our faith, as Peter would say, "to give an answer . . . a reason" (I Peter 3:15) for this article of our faith.

Maybe this cannot be done. Maybe it is sheer pride even to think of attempting it. Maybe we have no choice but to accept it by faith on the authority of the Bible and the Church. For this appears to be storming heaven itself and penetrating the very mysteries of God. Certainly the impure in heart or he who does not believe in Jesus Christ cannot do it. Certainly it cannot be done without the fullest illumination and assistance of the Holy Ghost. But it seems to me to be a perfectly indicated task especially in view of the spectacular progress of science and knowledge in general. Christians cannot just sit back and let this whole domain of science actualize itself outside the mastery and blessings of Christ. And I do not mean this only in the more or less political sense of Christianizing the scientists and making them pray to Christ and submit to His Law, or of sprinkling holy water upon scientific institutions and dedicating them to Christ. I mean an actual ontological demonstration in the order of being, not only of how Christ influenced history and is at the base of a great deal of culture, including perhaps scientific culture itself, but of how, even in this life, even while we must live by faith, even while we see only through a glass darkly, we can still somehow penetrate the darkness of faith and achieve a glimpse of how the Logos created everything, a glimpse into the very act of creation itself.

The German philosopher Kant emphasized the theoretical and moral nature of man and made everything in the universe depend on him. Hegel attempted a deduction of everything from pure reason which, regardless of what he said, was only the reason of man — in the end indeed, only of Hegel's own mind, and of yours and mine only to the extent we participate in Hegel's mind or "follow" his reasoning. The Communists emphasize man alone (in the sense of the collectivity) and want him to take everything into his own hands (in the sense of absolute political control), even to the extent of deriving all science and all culture, including religion and God, from the class struggle. The existentialists know nothing absolutely except man and his miserable existence. All right, then, here is this tremendous modern convergence upon man from every side. But we Christians have been affirming man ever since God himself became man. It is also clear that all these other affirmations of man owe their historical-cultural-existential possibility to this original Christian affirmation of man; indeed, they are so many corruptions of that affirmation. Could we not therefore show Kant, Hegel, the Communists, and the existentialists that their attempt to concentrate everything in and derive everything from man represents a sound instinct, but that it is our God-Man who is really the Alpha and Omega of all this impulse; Alpha, because He started it in the first place, whether directly or indirectly; and Omega, because the perfect man they pant after and long for and desire to create in history our God-Man already is? I will not press this line of thought; I am only suggesting it as an illustration.

The responsible demonstration of how through Jesus

Christ "all things were made" is a most ambitious project. It appears like hastening or illicitly anticipating the beatific vision which the faithful are promised only beyond the present veil of tears. But I believe we can part this veil a bit and take a peep into that vision even here. Real faith in Jesus Christ must involve some concern, some attempt at this demonstration. By its very nature, because He Himself is at stake in it, it can never succeed if its motive is silly curiosity, and if the heart, not having been washed of its sins by His blood, is not so pure as to be able to see God.

VII

I pass on to another domain in which our faith is tried. There is considerable softness and complacency unbecoming of a Christian. I do not mean Christians should not enjoy to the full the benefits of industrial civilization, especially as industrial civilization itself has arisen only in the bosom of Christian civilization. The creator of a thing is fully entitled to enjoy it. But we can be bewitched and beguiled by what we enjoy; we can become too dependent on it. And that is absolutely unchristian; that is idolatry; that is worshipping the creature rather than the Creator. It was not only the ancient Hebrews who constantly relapsed into idolatry; this seems to be an incurable trait in original human nature. Thus the sense of abundance could kill our faith; we may be tempted into feeling that we do not need faith; and then we cease to live by faith. And that is not just, for the just shall live by faith (Habakkuk 2:4, Romans 1:17, Galatians 3:11, Hebrews 10:38).

There is not enough spiritual tension, not enough self-stretching towards the end which is far away, not enough eschatology; while this is an age in which everything is eschatological, everything speaks of the end. People are quite satisfied with the world, and they seek and get more and more of the same kind of thing. There is not enough radical revulsion against the world and all its values, not enough reaching out with David towards God, not enough despair of the world, not enough passage to the other side. This worldliness, this trust in man and progress, this self-satisfaction and self-congratulation, this relaxed rest in culture and civilization and human values, is most inimical to the health of the spirit. It is like taking a Turkish bath and balmily relaxing all over, and forgetting God. This is sloth and covetousness, and I ask you to read Saint John Chrysostom on what happens to man when he is overcome by these afflictions.

We thus tend to think that this very culture and civilization in which we enjoy ourselves and take so much pride has created itself; that it subsists by itself and is self-sufficient. We thus lose sight of how much it owes Christ. There seems to be an inexorable fall in the nature of things, namely, that left to itself for long, without crisis and without judgment, the creature tends to forget the Creator. Man apparently cannot act except after God has acted; he cannot approach God except after God has approached him. This is perhaps the most original of all sins: the slothful inertia of being whereby the source and ground of all being is forgotten. Apparently as a creature you *must* fall in this original inertia; otherwise you would be the Creator Himself! Trial, temptation, suffering, chastening, death, the Cross, these then appear to be necessary in order to remind us who we are.

The life of slothfulness and satisfaction and relaxation

is certainly a life of death: try it and see what I mean; it makes you forget God, it causes you to tend in the end towards nothingness; for nothingness is exactly that where God is forgotten. Whatever the value of a relaxation of tensions in the international order, such a relaxation is disastrous in the order of the spirit. Nobody understands the mysterious depths of man and God who does not understand what James meant when he shouted: "Be afflicted, and mourn, and weep: let your laughter be turned to mourning, and your joy to heaviness" (James 4:9). In mourning and affliction we come much nearer to God than in laughter, and that is why they that mourn are called blessed, seeing that their reward is the comfort of God (Matthew 5:4).

VIII

The ecumenical movement provides another field for the testing of our faith. There is the National Council of the Churches of Christ in this country. There is the World Council of Churches. There is the Pope's announcement in 1959 that he would call an Ecumenical Council to examine, among other things, the question of unity, and now 1962 has been set for the convening of this Council. The Ecumenical Patriarch Athenagoras I has been working hard to see how the Orthodox Churches may be brought together and how the cause of general Christian unity may be furthered. Important discussions have been going on lately, in books, in magazines, and in private circles, on this theme. There is therefore an apparent urge among the Christians everywhere to see if they cannot come closer together.

Side by side with this there is an evident withdrawing of each communion into the sources of its own independent strength and belief, a tenacious if not a violent holding to what it knows and has received. A sincere urge towards unity, yes; but also a desperate clinging to your tradition lest you let go some truth that Christ has vouchsafed you. I myself can bear witness that I never was so conscious of the infinite wealth of what has been handed down to me in my own Orthodox tradition as I am now; and yet I pray day and night for the unity of those who have been baptized in the name of the Father, of the Son, and of the Holy Ghost.

Now this is a dialectical situation: in wishing and seeking unity we at the same time become exceedingly jealous of the trust which Christ has been pleased to commit to our keeping. I myself believe this is exactly as it should be. No unity based on sentiment or compromise or politics or human considerations is worthy of the Lord we know and worship. Besides, such a unity will never come about. We may seek and accept only the unity He wants. And therefore we cannot and we should not lightly yield on any matter that we honestly regard to be central to His will.

When such a dialectical situation arises, it is then that there is lots of hope. For the unity that is going to come about is not our making but His making. And God breaks through only in crisis; He speaks and acts only in tension. When all is smooth and well and there is no problem, why should He intervene? Herein comes our faith in Jesus Christ. It is a fact which will control all our further strivings that we were one up until 1054. We must therefore have faith that unity is His will and that He will consummate it in His own way and His own day precisely through the tension arising from each one of us holding firmly to what he knows and yet all of us yearning from the bottom of our hearts for the unity of the Body of our Lord. And I sometimes have the feeling that some people do not want unity, do not really believe in it, but rather feel that disunity is a good thing. What is needed therefore is faith, faith in unity, and I am sure Christ then will intervene.

I had the honor of speaking at length with Athenagoras I on this matter. I also had the honor of speaking at length with Pope John XXIII and the Cardinals most directly concerned. Finally, I had the honor of speaking at length with the leaders of the World Council of Churches and with other Protestant leaders. The following, then, constitute my present views and findings, for what they are worth, on this exceedingly pregnant moment in the history of the Church:

(1) The impulse to unity is genuine by all concerned: there is a refusal to take the existing disunity as a final and unalterable fact.

(2) People are attacking and suspecting each other much less, and their mood is: "We have had enough of this!"

(3) The Orthodox Churches have recently held important conferences among themselves, and there is some talk that some of the Churches of the East (the Coptic Church, for instance) will so redefine their position about the nature of our Lord that the Orthodox Church will then be able to accept them into her communion.

(4) Most intensive quiet studies and preparations are being carried out by the Roman Catholic Church on the whole question of unity.

(5) The World Council of Churches treated the question of unity as one of its major themes, both in the summer

of 1960 in Scotland and in its Third Assembly Session in New Delhi in the fall of 1961.

(6) If the new endeavors are tremendous, I assure you the old and new difficulties are also tremendous, and there is no power of darkness that will not be thrown afresh against Christ and His kingdom.

(7) It would appear that the least that Christ expects of us is to say nothing and do nothing and above all try to feel nothing that would hamper or obstruct the free workings of the Holy Spirit; to study and go deeply into this matter in all its aspects; to live in a positive state of expectancy of great things; and when definite proposals are put forward, not to reject them out of hand, but to turn them in our mind for months and years before we take a final decision on them.

It appears that faith in Jesus Christ involves faith in the unity of the Church. However I read the New Testament, the Fathers and the Creed, however I consider the history of the Church, and however I think of this question as to its essence, I come to the same conclusion. Disunity does not correspond to the will of Christ. Where it occurs — and it is a fact today — there is something wrong somewhere. And wrong in matters appertaining to Christ cannot be allowed. Our faith in Jesus Christ therefore is being tested today, negatively by how much we believe in Church unity, and positively by the role we shall play in the great opportunities which appear now to be opening up before us.

IX

Of course the greatest trial of our faith is we ourselves. We are trying God all the time. And His long-suffering

is simply incredible.   They talk of proofs for the existence
of God! We need no proof save the simple fact that
nobody and nothing can stand us; therefore, since nevertheless we are, there must be an infinite Being who does.
We exist; but we are impossible; therefore a Being must
exist to bear our impossibility for us; that Being is God.
The impossibility of man proves not only the possibility
but the absolute necessity of God. And, what is more, our
impossibility would have remained hidden from us (as
theirs is indeed from all those who do not know Him).
did He not choose to die, and nowhere save on the Cross
on a hill just outside Jerusalem, in order to reveal our
impossibility to us, and, in freedom, to make us possible and
bring us back to Himself.

You know how it is that in crises the best in us and the
worst in us comes to the fore at the same time. Everything
in us makes itself felt, the good and the bad. We are
like an undeveloped film, and a crisis is like the sun bringing out every little shade and light in our character. It is
when we see ourselves that we may lose our faith. It
is not that we would then cry with David, "My God,
my God, why hast thou forsaken me?" (Psalm 22:1).
Would that we did that! Would that we also added, "For
I have eaten ashes like bread, and mingled my drink with
weeping, because of thine indignation and thy wrath: for
thou has lifted me up, and cast me down" (Psalm 102:9,
10). It is that we might then cease to think of God
altogether. This is our greatest temptation, not our sin,
but that the devil, obsessing us with our sin, might succeed
in making us forget God and His infinite compassion.

Shall we then lose our faith in Jesus Christ because
the worst in us has made itself manifest together with

the best? What pride! Shall we lose our faith in Jesus Christ because our total personal truth has become crystal clear? I can only say with Paul, God forbid! I can only say with him, "I thank God through Jesus Christ our Lord" (Romans 7:25).

Frustration because of imperfection and sin? O yes! But thank God, Jesus Christ is without sin and He is our Lord. Only the Christian can say this. All others are just as sinful as, or they may even be much less sinful than, the Christians, but they do not have somebody to look up to who is without sin. It is not sin or sanctity that differentiates a Christian from a non-Christian; it is the Lord Jesus Christ whose mercy the poor Christian trusts. And you and I have known His power, how in the twinkling of an eye He is able to change everything and make us into a new creature. And then, "Eye hath not seen, nor ear heard, neither have entered into the heart of man, the things which God hath prepared for them that love him" (I Corinthians 2:9).

And so faith has been tested and through God's grace it has emerged triumphant over hell and the devil, when it can say with Paul, simply, quietly, and without guile: "For I am persuaded, that neither death, nor life, nor angels, nor principalities, nor powers, nor things present, nor things to come, nor height, nor depth, nor any other creature, shall be able to separate us from the love of God, which is in Christ Jesus our Lord" (Romans 8:38, 39).

CHAPTER VI

THE BURDEN OF THE CHRISTIAN

I

The Christian finds himself today thrown into a strange and difficult world, full of peril and anxiety. He knows Christ, he believes in Him, and he cannot forget what He has done for him in his own life. On the basis of this knowledge and faith he seeks to understand and to adjust to the terrible questions and uncertainties of the times. He knows it is unworthy of him as a Christian to bewail his fate and exaggerate the challenges in the midst of which he is thrown. Dangerous world? — yes. Unprecedented difficulties? — certainly. Tremendous challenges? — of course. But God does not love him less, nor has He singled him out for trial in a special furnace beyond his power to bear or to subdue. He remembers what Paul told the Corinthians and he understands it to be meant exactly for him: "God is faithful, who will not suffer you to be tempted above that ye are able; but will with the temptation also make a way to escape, that ye may be able to bear it" (I Corinthians 10:13). Every age has its own problems, every age its own burdens and complexities, and throughout man is fundamentally the same, able to know and rest in the truth or to rebel, and the devil precisely the same old adversary, with his sweetness and his wiles, and of course "Jesus Christ the same yesterday, and to day, and for ever" (Hebrews 13:8).

But if man and the devil and Christ are the same in every age, still every man lives in his own age and in no other, and faces his own problems and carries his own cross which no other man can possibly face or carry for him. We have this one life to live which is absolutely unique and absolutely our own. This is not the decaying Athenian world which Socrates would rather die than adjust to, nor the Roman world at its highest splendor which Paul had to contend with and utilize in the service of the Gospel, nor this same world at its last gasp for which Augustine wrote the epitaph in his magnificent *City of God,* nor the Hellenistic world at Antioch to which Chrysostom preached his inimitable homilies, nor the rotten world of the eleventh century at the time of the Great Schism between East and West, nor the exuberant world of the fifteenth and sixteenth centuries when limitless horizons began to beckon the energies of men, nor the world of the nineteenth century when Western Europe held under its sway virtually all mankind. We are not called upon to live in any of these worlds, although our indebtedness to the great scholars who actually live in thought in them and lovingly reproduce them to us is incalculable. But even these our benefactors see and interpret the past from the only vantage point accessible to them, namely, from this one common world to which they and we belong. Every man must work out his own destiny, meet his own fate, carry his own burden, come to terms with himself and with God, from within the one and unique world into which he has been flung.

What, then, is the burden of the Christian today, the Christian who, as a man, shares the same humanity with David and Socrates and Paul and Augustine, this very humanity over which the devil and Jesus Christ are engaged in eternal combat, and yet who must carry on this warfare of the soul in this very age, the age of the cold war and the nuclear bomb, the age of the infinite wonders of science, and the age in which every people on earth is demanding as never before the right to some place under the sun?

Before I endeavor to answer this question I must first say one word about the essence of the Christian, for we are speaking here, not of the burden of the American or the European or the capitalist or the wage earner, but the burden of the Christian. We are assuming the existence of a distinct being called "the Christian."

The Christian is defined by a kind of love: the Christian loves Jesus Christ above everything else. This love is not an ordinary act of the will on his part, as for instance when we decide to read a book or to take a trip abroad or to attend a meeting or to pay a visit to a friend. The dawning of Christ's love is not something we conjure up ourselves. We love Jesus Christ only when we realize how much He loved us, and indeed loved us without first seeking or receiving our consent. Thus our love of Jesus Christ is a pale reflection of His love for us.

II

On the basis of this existing love of Jesus Christ above everything else — and if it does not exist, then we are talking about something else — the following appear to me to constitute the burden of the Christian today.

The Christian lives at the heart of the great issues of our day: he hates existing at the periphery of life. Nationalism, socialism, science, war and peace, the demands of justice, the international order, the miraculous contraction of the world, the conflicting ideologies that compete for men's allegiance — the Christian penetrates to the essence of these things as much as he can, certainly more than anybody else. Nothing that stirs men at the center of their life is foreign to his mind. Where there is being, where there is decision, where there is determination of events, there the Christian is, at least in interest and concern. For he knows that Jesus Christ has a will for all that.

The Christian seeks to know the facts. This is not easy these days, with so much hearsay, sentimentalism, and prejudice; and so he cannot be too wary against propaganda and falsehood. Nothing is more comfortable than to be swept with the current, especially when the current is so strong; but a Christian fights stupidity, superficiality and tendentiousness like hell. There is truth, his duty is to seek it, and his destiny is to find it and feed on it. The difference between the attitude of the Christian and that of so many others is that, whereas others may wish to transform the nature of things to suit their own purposes, the Christian only wishes to discover that nature so as to conform to it himself. Their attitude is more one of will and power; his attitude is more one of understanding and love.

It follows that he sees through the silly slogans and stupid shibboleths. It is appalling how much we are daily bombarded with *clichés* and how much we actually live

on them. We repeat such things as "the free world,"
"Western civilization," "nuclear parity," "nuclear holo-
caust," "coexistence," "neutral government," "economic
development," "socialism," "international understanding,"
"social justice," "human rights," "practical and impractical,"
"independence," "justice," "peace," "freedom," not to mention a host of other matters taken from the fields of psychology and other special sciences. And not only do we
repeat these things as though we understood them, but
we draw all sorts of conclusions, as to attitude and expectation and policy, that do not, on a strict view of things,
follow from them at all. Nothing is more heroic today
— and existence today is as heroic as it was in any age in
in the past — than the spiritual struggle against the deception of words and the distortion of meanings and the
bondage of *clichés*. The Christian carries out this struggle
all the more cheerfully because he knows — and this
knowledge is daily verified for him — that the Lord whom
he loves is "the way, the truth, and the life" and "in him
is no darkness at all" (John 14:6 and I John 1:5).

It follows also that the Christian today desperately prays
that he be given the power to distinguish the false from
the true prophets. Does a day pass without somebody
coming forward with his own method or system or plan
or "doctrine" or "way" or "pet idea" or "answer" for the
salvation of the world? You need men with a special
charisma, they tell you, to cope with the problems of
Asia and Africa; and such-and-such a man, ah! he got it!
With such profusion of proposal, prophecy and person, are
we not in danger of being completely lost? And so when
the Christian thinks of the words of Christ: "For there

shall arise false Christs, and false prophets, and shall shew great signs and wonders; insomuch that, if it were possible, they shall deceive the very elect" (Matthew 24:24; see also Matthew 7:15, Mark 13:22 and I John 4:1) — when he thinks of these words, he begins to fear and tremble lest he be deceived! And at once he remembers the other words of Scripture: ". . . believe not every spirit, but try the spirits whether they are of God" (I John 4:1). How shall he try them? How can he guard against deception? To answer this is indeed to beg the question. For if one suggests a special sure "method," he will be suggesting another dubious "way." Thus there is in reality only the given rule: "Not by might, nor by power, but by my spirit, saith the Lord of hosts" (Zechariah 4:6). Therefore no mechanical method avails here: there is only the Holy Spirit Himself who will "try the spirits" and "guide [us] into all truth" (John 16:13). We can only pray: "Come, Holy Spirit." What we may say, however, is that whatever conduces only to the glory of man or some other creature is false; and we may confidently affirm that that prophet alone is true and that answer alone is right that conduces in the end somehow to the glory of God.

III

A Christian thrown into the present world cannot subscribe to any international order just because it affords him a sense of peace and relieves him of the necessity of hard moral decisions. What if the sense of peace were false and illusory? How can he be sure it will not be shattered? What is at stake here is justice, truth, and man. Thus an order that is not based on natural justice, on the dignity of man, and on the trust of truth to vindicate itself, cannot flow from the mind of Christ, nor can it merit His love.

War is terrible, and not only will a Christian not provoke it, but he will do everything in his power to prevent it from breaking out. But six things do not follow from this: (a) it does not follow that if war is forced upon him he will not defend himself; (b) nor does it follow that he will not in advance prepare to defend himself, since there is nothing to guarantee that war will not be forced upon him; (c) nor does it follow that if and when war is forced upon him he will not fight like a man or will not fight for complete victory; (d) nor does it follow that, since cold war is a kind of war, he will not fight it to victory; (e) nor does it follow that under conditions of war, whether cold or hot, he will blaspheme God and cease to be a Christian, loving Christ above everything else and his neighbor as himself; (f) nor, finally, does it follow that, if he is opposed to war, he has any right to be opposed only to that form of war which is "international," namely, war between the nations, while saying nothing whatsoever about that other form of war which goes by the name of "class war," namely, war between social and economic classes which could be just as terrible and just as unjust and just as devastating as any so-called "international war." It is pride and lack of faith to turn to God and say to Him: "Look here, I can only live the Christian life under conditions of peace!" What if you are tried precisely under conditions of war! Would you then follow Job's wife's advice and "curse God, and die" (Job 2:9)? Is it not prudent to prepare even for such a trial? Nothing is more certain from the Christian point of view than that only he who is spiritually prepared to acquit himself honorably under the most trying conditions, including conditions of war, is entitled to enjoy the blessings of peace.*

If a Christian faces movements and tendencies that negate Christ and seek to destroy Him, he cannot sit back and do nothing: he must react. He cannot say: it is none of my business, Christ will take care of Himself! Our world is full of such movements and tendencies. Because nothing less than his faith is at stake, the Christian is called upon to witness to his faith perhaps as never before. We really know the grace wherein we stand only when we are pricked in our heart by Christ's tremendous saying: "Whosoever therefore shall be ashamed of me and of my words in this adulterous and sinful generation; of him also shall the Son of man be ashamed, when he cometh in the glory of his Father with the holy angels" (Mark 8:38; Luke 9:26). It will be a separate task to work out the many and strange and subtle ways in which this shame expresses itself these days.

IV

Just as every creature of God has a goodness and a being all its own, so no one of man's creations is devoid of some goodness, some truth. Every people, every culture,

*I am aware of the intense interest which questions of war and peace have aroused in America and throughout the world. The various schools of pacifists have helped more than any other people to focus interest on this issue. I for one am grateful to them for their vigorous discussion and their unrelenting challenge. In addition to what I have briefly indicated above, the reader can find, if he is interested in my views, further amplifications of them in an article entitled "Christian Morals in International Affairs," which appeared in the *Harvard Divinity Bulletin* of July, 1960, and in a small piece entitled "Freedom Must Win," which appeared in the *Presbyterian Outlook* of October 9, 1961.

every outlook has something to say, no matter how much it may otherwise be pervaded with darkness and error. In an age in which every human creation appears to be goaded to assert itself, the Christian is particularly called upon to be big enough and fair enough to recognize in his heart and life every bit of truth and every reflection of being wherever he may find them and regardless of the mountains of dross in which they may be buried. To be fair, to be positive, to be thankful — these are highly desirable Christian virtues today. And of course you are not fair at all if, in trying to be fair to others, you are so fair as to cease to be fair to Christ Himself — Christ who was much more than just fair to you and me when He took our sins upon Himself on the Cross.

In the New Testament there are a dozen or more striking listings of the sins of that age. (See, e.g., Matthew 15:19, Mark 7:21-22, Romans 1:29-31, I Corinthians 6:9ff., II Corinthians 6:4ff., Galatians 5:19ff., Ephesians 4:31 and 5:3-4, Philippians 4:8 — by way of opposites —, Colossians 3:5, I Timothy 1:9ff. and 6:4ff., II Timothy 3:2ff., Titus 3:1ff., I Peter 2:1 and 4:3, and Revelation 21:8 and 22:15.) All these sins are rampant today. But we may add as peculiar to our age: hecticness, nervousness, fear, cowardice, sheer rebellion, absence of rest and peace, the flattening of thought and feeling, the absence of the dimension of depth, the denial of the higher and lower, the innumerable new ways in which pleasure can be safely stolen, the disintegration of community, the absence of roots, the rise of the irrational and dark and massive, the spread of many magical cults, the rise of superstition, reliance upon speculation and chance, the disdain of the law of cause and effect, the weakening of the sense of personal responsibility, the denial of the invisible and spiritual, the spread of militant atheism, the proud self-sufficiency of man and culture. His is as heroic a life as any in history who lives through and emerges from all this with the integrity of his soul not irreparably damaged, and with his heart still "faithful to the heavenly vision." With all his bruises he can at least trust himself to the mercy of God.

V

The Christian cannot possibly be thankful enough to all those throughout the ages who through their faithfulness and suffering passed on the light of Christ from man to man and generation to generation until it finally shone upon his face. There is nothing he can do even to begin to demonstrate his gratitude. But they really want nothing from him except to be faithful in turn to what he knows and believes. Let the light then never dim or darken; let it pass on interminably, always replenished, according to God's will, with new power from above. The unbroken passing on of the light of the countenance of Christ is the essence of the missionary movement, and while much that is good has come out of America, nothing better or deeper or more lasting has radiated from this land than this mighty witness to Christ. In their own quiet and humble way, the American churches have helped, as much as any other endeavor, in awakening and enlightening whole regions of the globe. All glory and honor and peace to those who labored in this vineyard, who shall certainly see the face of the Lamb — the Lamb whose name shall certainly be in their foreheads (Revelation 22:4). Witnessing to Christ, suffering for His name, passing on His light, mediating His salvation, building the household of God, preaching the Word to the four corners of the earth — this *mission* of the Church is more urgent and more necessary today than ever before.

The Christian today is called upon to rediscover the wholeness of the Christian tradition. There is in this discovery more excitement, more challenge, more reward than in any other adventure. And the opportunities are simply unprecedented; for when could the honest seeker have available to him half as much excellent literature on all aspects of Christian faith and history as he has today; and when could Christians all over the world see each other and discover each other and learn from each other half as readily as they can today; and when were they subjected in their faith and in their hope to corrosive doubt from within and radical onslaught from without half as aggressively as they are today? There is therefore a providential preparation on all sides for the current ecumenical impulse. Despite all human recalcitrance, unity is in the air! I assure you I have a firsthand knowledge of the difficulties; but I am like a child: I trust the Holy Ghost to be stronger than any difficulty. And — who knows?! — He may still surprise the most skeptical among us.

VI

Beyond every burden and care, the Christian has his own soul to worry about. Oh yes, he is honest and upright, he works hard, he reads the Bible, he meditates on the saints, he has his times of profound prayer and retreat to the depths, he lives an active Church life, he takes an humble part in the stirring spiritual movements of the day, he is alive to the problems

of the world, he is as good and solid a citizen as any
other person, and, above all, he develops ulcers, those
peculiar *stigmata* of our age! But, is he the master of
his own passions? How much does he know the living
power of God in his own life — that power which is
much more than the *daimon* of Socrates which only warns
and forbids, that power which also directs and constitutes
and provides? Is he at peace with himself? Is he true
to himself? Is he true to Christ? How much does Christ
come to his rescue exactly in time? In his daily wrestlings
with the devil, does he spit in his face and trample his
head under foot — not in his own power, but always
in the power of the Cross? Has he forgiven his brother —
really forgiven him? Is all rancor and resentment washed
away by the blood of Christ? How else can he hope for
the forgiveness of God of which he stands in such desperate
need?

Beyond every other care and worry, the Christian carries
these questions on his mind all the time, and with them
he transcends his turbulent age and becomes one with all
ages in which the same ultimate questions tormented the
saints. It is reconciliation and peace with God that he
craves for more than anything else. It is that life of
closeness to God, that intimacy of living with Christ, that
mighty infusion of the Holy Ghost, which is absolute
light, absolute certainty, absolute power. In this state
which he craves for, which he believes in, which he confidently expects, having been promised it by One who does
not lie, the Christian attains that divine *sophia* in which
the tongue is untied and from which everything else flows.
The Christian has a foretaste of this even in this life.
There is then courage, there is communion, there is peace,

there is the fellowship of the pure, of those who have seen God.

Now our present life is interesting and let no one belittle its duties and challenges and excitements. Moreover, these are great days and what is being decided in them is absolutely historic. But all these things are going to pass, and with them life itself. What, then, is the life that does not pass, what, then, is life eternal? This is the first and last question. And all I know is that I am told and I believe that "this is life eternal, that they might know thee the only true God, and Jesus Christ whom thou hast sent" (John 17:3).

CHAPTER VII

UNITY AND HISTORY

I

The problem of Christian unity is inseparable from the problem of the Church. Christian unity is in effect Church unity. For some Christians can claim that in some vague sense they are already "united" with all other Christians in that they all have a special relationship to Jesus Christ. It is therefore the nature and authority of the Church that is here in question. Unity is fundamentally determined by ecclesiology.

This raises in turn the problem of God's relations to history, and indeed the problem of the nature of history itself. How does God act in history? How has He acted? Do we just get up every morning, read the Bible, say our prayers, and then God, there and then, directly deals with us, independently of anything in the past, independently even of His past dealings with other men? Or is there a meaning and a reality to the authentic transmission of the tradition from generation to generation and culture to culture? How has the past mediated God to us? What is the content of human historical solidarity? What is the content of the divine historical economy? Concretely, what do we owe the past? And this very Bible, where did it come from? Who has certified its revealed character? Our theories of unity and history therefore mutually determine each other.

Ecclesiology and what I might term "historiology" are at the base of any serious quest for Christian unity. Seek first the nature of the Church and the nature of history, and the problem of Christian unity becomes perfectly clear to you. What did Christ intend the Church *to be* and how has this intended being *actually existed in history?* — these are the two ultimate questions. The truth of these two questions does not arise from any arbitrary decision: the truth positively and independently exists, and, if humbly sought, can be ascertained.

II

In a very real sense unity reigned until 1054. Two questions then must be answered: what was it that constituted that unity while it lasted, and what happened when the Great Schism between East and West occurred? No man can answer these two questions *a priori;* he must make use of the excellent existing historical and doctrinal studies.

Since Christ certainly wants unity, it is not reasonable to suppose that the unity that once reigned for a thousand years did not answer to the will of Christ. Therefore the pattern of that unity must serve as our norm. We are not starting from zero wondering what the will of Christ is: we have a thousand years behind us — and therefore "before" us — of actual, concrete manifestation of that will.

This raises the question of doctrinal evolution since then. This is a very difficult question, but those who sincerely put unity above every other consideration, except the consideration of the truth, and conformity to the will of Christ, will not fail, with the help of the Holy Ghost, to find ways and means for solving even this most crucial question. I have proposals on this point, but who am I to make them? By its very nature this problem can be handled only between duly constituted authorities of corporate churches.

The craving for unity and the pressure of the Holy Ghost to that end are among the clearest phenomena of this age. In importance I place this matter above every other contemporary excitement. It follows that no problem connected with the question of unity is too delicate to be faced and discussed: everything must be lifted into the open, everything must be humbly gone into — the tradition, the Bible, the Councils, the Pope, the question of the episcopacy, the heirarchy, the liturgy, the Protestant principles, the teaching authority of the Church, cultural and political matters — absolutely everything.

People rightly worry about all sorts of terrible problems today, but let the Christians constitute one real Body of Christ, and no problem then will be beyond their power to solve or to control.

Absolute understanding, absolute humility, absolute charity, utter patience and the total overcoming of the pride and self-will of man by the grace and love of Jesus Christ — without these no unity can be achieved or maintained. But these things are well within the power of the Holy Ghost.

Those who, having been baptized in the name of the Father and the Son and the Holy Ghost, love Jesus Christ above everything else, and, while unworthy, nevertheless seek to obey Him, live under the necessity of wholeheartedly praying and working for unity according to His will. The believer can aspire to no greater reward than to be granted to see a measure of true unity realized in his lifetime.